Eliot Attridge and Bob Woodcc

ESSENTIALS
OCR GCSE
Biology A

Contents

Unit A161

3 Module B1: You and Your Genes
13 Module B2: Keeping Healthy
24 Module B3: Life on Earth

Unit A162

34 Module B4: The Processes of Life
45 Module B5: Growth and Development
56 Module B6: Brain and Mind

Unit A163

68 Module B7: Further Biology (Peak Performance)
83 Further Biology (Learning from Ecosystems)
91 Further Biology (New Technologies)

1–12 Answers (found at the centre of the book)

You and Your Genes B1

1. Read the following newspaper article.

   ### Little Sleep for Mexican Blind Cave Fish

   In April, 2011, biologists reported in the journal, *Cell*, that Mexican Blind Cave Fish had evolved the capacity to cope with less sleep than the surface variety of the fish. They had observed that surface fish clearly slept at night, having been found inactive at the bottom of the laboratory tank with their fins drooping. The variants that were found in caves, however, patrolled the laboratory tanks all night. The temperature of the water in the tanks was kept constant.

   The researchers allowed the two variants to breed and studied the behaviour of their offspring.

	% Sleeping at Night	% Awake at Night
Surface fish	100	0
Cave fish	0	100
Hybrid offspring	40	60

   (a) Which of the following is **not** a possible hypothesis for the experiment? Put a tick (✓) in the box next to the correct answer. [1]

   There will be a difference in the offspring due to pH. ☐

   There will be a difference in the offspring due to the water temperature. ☐

   There will be a difference in the offspring due to the air quality. ☐

   There will be a difference in the offspring due to the amount of light. ☐

   (b) The researchers were sure that their evidence showed that the trait for coping with a lack of sleep was inherited. What evidence did they have to show this? [1]

   (c) If 250 offspring were born during the experiment, calculate how many offspring would be awake at night. Show your working. [2]

   (d) The researchers used 12 of each type of fish. What could you say to criticise this experiment and, consequently, how could you improve it? [1]

   (e) The researchers hypothesised that the cave fish did not necessarily need less sleep. Instead they believed the cave fish needed to stay awake more to allow them to catch more food, which in a cave may be scarce. What aspect of Ideas about Science does this represent? Put a tick (✓) in the box next to the **best** answer. [1]

   Thinking creatively ☐   Thinking scientifically ☐

   Thinking quickly ☐   Thinking abstractly ☐

B1 You and Your Genes

2. Spinal Muscular Atrophy (SMA) is a **recessive** disease that causes the nerve cells of sufferers to degenerate.

   (a) If the symbol for the recessive allele is **a**, what will the alleles be in a person who does **not** carry the disorder? [1]

   (b) Look at the family tree below showing the inheritance of SMA in a family.

   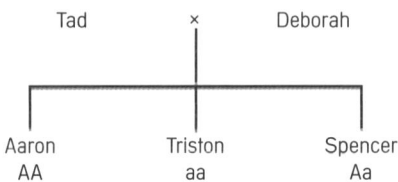

   What alleles are carried by…

   Tad? .... Deborah? .... [1]

   (c) Spencer married Alev. Alev has no family history of SMA. They want to have children. Explain the chances of them having a child with the disorder. Why is it useful to be able to test adults for the presence of harmful alleles and what are the risks?

   ✎ The quality of written communication will be assessed in your answer to this question. [6]

3. Genetic diseases, such as Huntington's disease and cystic fibrosis, have symptoms. Draw straight lines from each of the genetic diseases to their symptoms. [4]

Disease	Symptom	Disease
Huntington's	Memory loss	Cystic fibrosis
	Difficulty digesting food	
	Mood changes	
	Difficulty breathing	

You and Your Genes — B1

4. **(a)** Read the following article about predictive testing for genetic diseases.

> ### Is Predictive Testing the Answer?
>
> **1** There are many genetic disorders that afflict people around the world.
>
> **2** It is now possible to test adults, children and embryos to see if they carry a faulty allele.
>
> **3** In the case of embryo testing, there are two genetic tests: chorionic villus sampling and amniocentesis.
>
> **4** With both of these tests, there is a chance that having the test will cause the premature death of the embryo.
>
> **5** Each year, 1 in 200 amniocentesis tests ends in the miscarriage of the pregnancy.
>
> **6** Some people argue that we should not end the lives of unborn children in this way; others argue that it prevents suffering in the future.

   (i) Which **two** sentences contain a statement about risk? Write the numbers of the sentences. [1]

   ....

   (ii) Which sentence, **1, 2, 3, 4, 5** or **6**, gives a statistic about risk? [1]

   ....

   (b) Which of the following measures of risk is the highest? Put a ring around the correct answer. [1]

       1 in 20   **1 in 5**   **1 in 100**   **1 in 1000**   **2 in 40**

5. Some friends are discussing 'designer babies'.

Samuel
Altering DNA is unnatural. It is against God.

Damiie
I'd only like to have male babies.

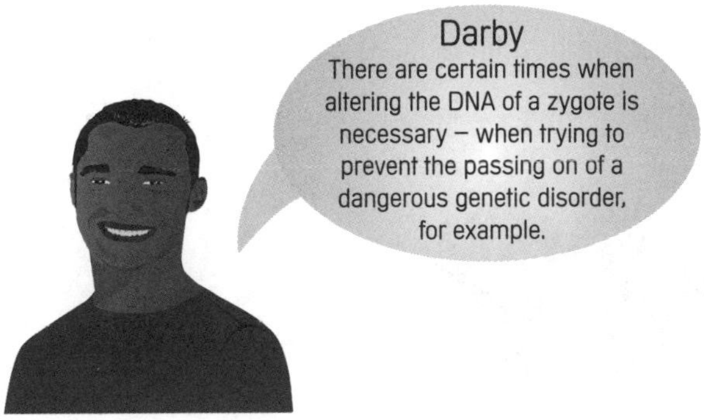

Darby
There are certain times when altering the DNA of a zygote is necessary – when trying to prevent the passing on of a dangerous genetic disorder, for example.

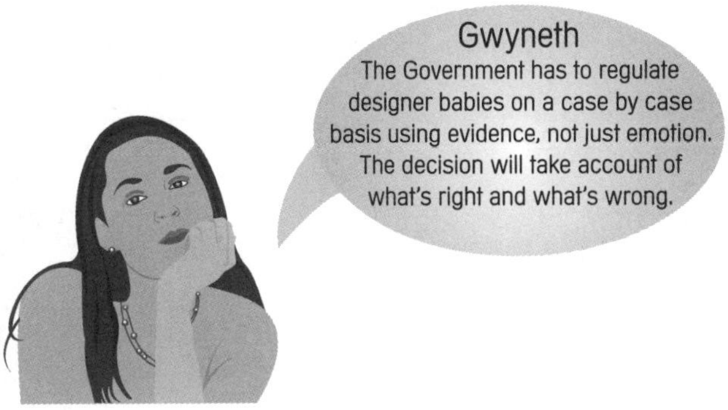

Gwyneth
The Government has to regulate designer babies on a case by case basis using evidence, not just emotion. The decision will take account of what's right and what's wrong.

B1 You and Your Genes

(a) Who has made a statement which gives a scientific reason for allowing designer babies? [1]

....

(b) Who has made a statement which indicates that ethics have to be considered? [1]

....

6. A study suggests that shoe size increases with a student's intelligence between the ages of 4 and 16.

(a) Why would it be wrong to try to increase a student's shoe size in an attempt to improve their intelligence? Put ticks (✓) in the boxes next to the **two** correct statements. [2]

Adult shoes have extra tax on them. It is better to keep to smaller shoes to save money. ☐

Although there is a correlation, it does not necessarily mean that there is also a cause. ☐

As children grow, their feet grow too. In addition, as they grow their brains will develop more. ☐

It's the other way round: improving intelligence leads to bigger feet. ☐

(b) In a class of students, the range of shoe sizes is from size 1 to size 12. On the axes below draw the line graph that you would expect to get if the shoe sizes were measured and plotted. Label the y-axis. [2]

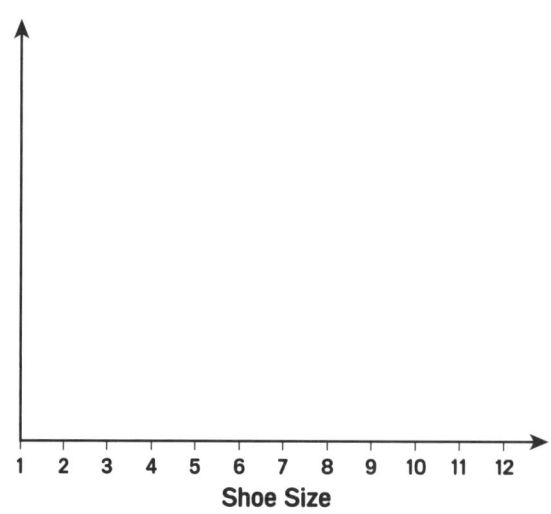

7. In 2010 in the UK, identical quads went to school for the first time.

You and Your Genes — B1

(a) Which statement explains how identical quads are formed? Put a tick (✓) in the box next to the correct statement. [1]

One egg was fertilised by four sperm. ☐

Two eggs were both fertilised by a sperm and then they both separated. ☐

One egg was fertilised by one sperm which then divided and separated once. ☐

One egg was fertilised by one sperm which divided once and then separated, and then each cell divided and separated again. ☐

(b) The quads will share certain features. Which statement will definitely be correct throughout the quads' lives? Put a tick (✓) in the box next to the correct statement. [1]

They will have the same fingerprints. ☐

The way their ear lobes are attached will be the same. ☐

They will have the same allergies. ☐

They will like the same music. ☐

(c) The chance of giving birth to identical quads is given as 1 in 64 000 000. Explain what the **1 in 64 000 000** statement means. [2]

....

....

....

(d) Although the quads look the same, their parents can recognise them. Why is this so? Put a tick (✓) in the box next to the **best** statement. [1]

The quads have different names. ☐

The environment causes subtle differences. ☐

Some genes are always different. ☐

Their fingerprints are different. ☐

[Total: .... / 32]

B1 You and Your Genes

Higher Tier

8. Monosodium Glutamate (MSG) is a chemical flavouring often added to Asian foods, such as Chinese and Japanese meals. It adds the umami flavour to food. It is caused by the body tasting the molecule glutamate, which is found naturally in tomatoes, mushrooms and broccoli.

A small number of people are not able to taste the chemical. This is due to a taste receptor, known as TASR1, being faulty.

The gene that codes for the TASR1 receptor responsible for MSG recognition is given as M.

(a) State the **genotype** for a heterozygous individual. [1]

(b) State the **phenotype** of a person with mm alleles. [1]

(c) If someone is a carrier for the allele and has children with another carrier, what is the chance of having a baby who is…

  (i) a carrier? [1]

  (ii) homozygous recessive and so unable to taste MSG? [1]

  (iii) completely free of the condition? [1]

(d) If someone is a carrier for the allele and has children with another carrier, what would the ratio of…

  (i) the genotypes be? [1]

  (ii) the phenotypes be? [1]

You and Your Genes — B1

9. Adele was 16 when she discovered that she did not carry the sex-determining region Y (SRY) gene. She had assumed that the fact that she had never had a period had been due to having polycystic ovaries, which her sister has. However, after seeing her doctor and having a genetic test, she discovered that she did not carry the SRY gene.

Which statements about Adele's condition are scientifically correct? Put ticks (✓) in the boxes next to the **two** correct statements. [2]

Adele has the body type of a female, including uterus, fallopian tubes, cervix and vagina. ☐

Adele has the sex chromosomes XXY. ☐

Adele has the sex chromosomes XY. ☐

Adele's body cannot detect the hormone androgen. ☐

10. Explain the procedure for pre-implantation genetic diagnosis (PGD). Suggest what the ethical issues are with this technique.

✎ *The quality of written communication will be assessed in your answer to this question.* [6]

_____

_____

_____

_____

_____

_____

11. Embryonic stem cells are seen as having the potential to cure many genetic diseases. Which statements best describe embryonic stem cells? Put ticks (✓) in the boxes next to the **three best** statements. [2]

Embryonic stem cells…

…can be taken up to the 40th day of pregnancy. ☐

…can only be taken from an embryo up to the 8 cell stage. ☐

…can be harvested from any part of the body. ☐

…have the potential to become any cell type. ☐

…are unspecialised cells. ☐

B1 You and Your Genes

12. A group of students is discussing whether the Government should force people to have genetic tests.

April
Having a genetic test will help to target illnesses earlier. It can only help to save lives.

Jonathan
But genetic testing would mean that you may not get insured! If you carry a gene for coronary heart disease, it doesn't mean that you will get it.

Matthew
If the information fell into the wrong hands it could be terrible.

Skirmante
You could be tested to check if a drug is likely to work on you. That could prevent suffering.

(a) Which **two** students are suggesting benefits of genetic testing? [1]

_____ and _____

(b) Which **two** students are suggesting negative consequences? [1]

_____ and _____

You and Your Genes — B1

13. Read this newspaper article.

> ### Testing for Intolerance
>
> At some stage in our lives we may need to take medicinal drugs. The problem is that drugs are developed and tested on relatively small numbers of individuals.
>
> Unfortunately, some of us may suffer side effects, for example some painkillers can cause stomach ulcers.
>
> Sometimes drugs will not even work as the patient does not have the correct receptor for the drug to work.
>
> The advent of genetic testing promises to usher in an era of personalised medicine. Patients will be able to take only those drugs that will work for them and have minimal side effects.

(a) Explain what is meant by **personalised medicine** and why knowing what genetic variants are carried is so important for deciding what drugs a patient is given. [3]

(b) Genetic tests can have a variety of outcomes. Considering these, give two potential problems that can arise when using genetic testing to see if you are likely to suffer from side effects and either benefit or not benefit from a drug. [2]

(c) The Government could make it the law that you **have** to have your genome screened and stored on a genetic database. It would then be a simple process to determine whether a drug is suitable or not. Give one argument why this may not be a good idea. [1]

B1 You and Your Genes

14. Read the newspaper article.

From Frogs to Dolly

Dolly the sheep was the first mammal to be cloned from adult body cells. Before Dolly, scientists had been trying to obtain clones from other animals. It was very difficult: how could you prove that the new organism was a clone?

In 1952, frogs were cloned by scientists. They took green frogs and extracted their eggs. The DNA was removed and DNA from albino frog tadpoles was introduced. When the frogs grew up, they were all albino.

In 1997, an egg from a black-faced ewe was taken and the DNA from the mammary gland of a Finn Dorset ewe was introduced. After electrical stimulation the egg started to divide and form an embryo.

Eventually, one of the eggs successfully grew into the sheep known as Dolly. However, out of 217 embryos, Dolly was the only one that successfully grew into an adult sheep. She died six years later.

(a) Suggest why using animals with very different looks from the donor of the egg are used. [1]

(b) Calculate the percentage efficiency of the technique that led to Dolly. Show your working. [2]

(c) Unlike cloning mammals such as Dolly the sheep, cloning humans is banned by international law. Some people, however, would argue that we should be able to allow cloning. Discuss the arguments for and against cloning humans.

The quality of written communication will be assessed in your answer to this question. [6]

(d) To date it has only been possible to clone frogs, unlike mammals such as Dolly, from embryonic cells. What conclusion can be made? Put a tick (✓) in the box next to the **best** answer. [1]

Frogs are more advanced organisms. ☐

DNA degenerates over time. ☐

Not all genomes of adult cells can lead to the development of a new organism. ☐

It is a complete mystery which scientists will never solve. ☐

[Total: ____ / 35]

Keeping Healthy B2

1. This question is about the immune system.

   (a) Which statement about the immune system below is **incorrect**? Put a tick (✓) in the box next to the answer. [1]

   Some white blood cells hunt for microorganisms in the body. ☐

   Microorganisms have antibodies on their surface. ☐

   White blood cells can engulf microorganisms. ☐

   Memory cells use antibodies to detect and kill the microorganism. ☐

   (b) A scientist has announced to the press that he has discovered a new cell in the immune system. He has not yet published his results. Which is the **best** reason why other scientists may be sceptical about his statement? Put a tick (✓) in the box next to the best answer. [1]

   The scientist is not necessarily an expert in his field. ☐

   He is only in it for the fame. ☐

   Other scientists have not been able to check his results. ☐

   The immune system is already completely understood. ☐

2. A new bleach says that it kills '99.99% of bacteria'.

   (a) If there were 1 000 000 bacteria in your toilet, how many would be left immediately after treating it with the bleach? Show your working. [2]

   _____

   _____

   (b) The doubling time of the bacteria in the toilet is 30 minutes. What is the maximum number of bacteria after cleaning the toilet and then leaving it for 5 hours? Show your working. [2]

   _____

   _____

   _____

   (c) Give **three** conditions that aerobic bacteria need to survive. [3]

   1. _____

   2. _____

   3. _____

B2 Keeping Healthy

3. In 2010, a scientific study carried out by the Food Standards Agency showed that 65.2% of all chickens sold in supermarkets was contaminated with *Campylobacter* – the cause of the majority of food-poisoning cases in the UK.

Cooking chicken thoroughly and washing areas that have come into contact with the raw meat kills *Campylobacter*. Each year, 400 000 people get food poisoning from *Campylobacter* and 80 people die. *Campylobacter* can be treated with antibiotics.

(a) Assuming that the UK population is 61 000 000, calculate the following. Show your working.

    (i) The percentage of the population that gets food poisoning from *Campylobacter*. [2]

    (ii) The percentage of the population that dies from *Campylobacter* food poisoning. [2]

    (iii) Why is it important to know the difference between these figures? [1]

(b) Why would it be wrong to say that chickens cause 400 000 people to get *Campylobacter* food poisoning each year? Put ticks (✓) in the boxes next to the **two best** answers. [2]

There is a correlation, which means there is a cause. ☐

There is a correlation, which only suggests that there may be a cause. ☐

There are other sources of *Campylobacter*. ☐

Campylobacter is a virus and can be found everywhere. ☐

(c) Astra is worried by the study. She believes that the risk is so great that she will not eat meat any more. Many people make decisions in similar ways every day. Explain why her decision not to eat meat is not necessarily a good idea and why people make mistakes understanding risk.

    ✎ *The quality of written communication will be assessed in your answer to this question.* [6]

Keeping Healthy B2

4. MMR is a vaccine that protects against three dangerous diseases: mumps, measles and rubella (German measles). Some friends are discussing vaccination.

Siobhan
I am not going to chance giving my daughter the MMR vaccine. She may get autism. Although there's a risk of getting the diseases, it's not worth it.

Salma
Everyone else is vaccinated. There's no need for me to get my children vaccinated.

Spencer
My grandad lost his twin sister at the age of 12 and he became blind, all because they caught measles.

Ian
No-one has measles nowadays. There's no point having the vaccine.

(a) Three of the friends have underestimated the risk that can occur from not having the vaccine. Who has **not** made this mistake? [1]

_____

(b) Who is confusing the small risk of a side effect with the much larger risk of catching the disease? [1]

_____

(c) Who is relying on a large enough pool of vaccinated people to keep the disease at bay? [1]

_____

B2 Keeping Healthy

(d) Some people argue that vaccination is not worth the risk. Explain how vaccination works and suggest what problems may happen when too few people are vaccinated.

✏ The quality of written communication will be assessed in your answer to this question. [6]

....

....

....

....

....

....

....

5. Complete the following sentences. Use words from this list. [4]

liquids   bacteria   viruses   chemicals   kill   grow

Antimicrobials are .... that .... bacteria, fungi and viruses.

Antibiotics are a type of antimicrobial which are only effective against .... They

are not effective against ...., which is why you are not given them when you

have flu.

6. Tuberculosis (TB) is a disease caused by a bacterium. Read the newspaper article and then answer the questions that follow.

TB – Could it Return?

A The vaccine BCG, which protects against the killer disease tuberculosis (TB), ceased to be given routinely to children in the UK in 2005.

B BCG was 80% effective against the bacterium that causes TB.

C Having the vaccine resulted in a painful blister on the arm that eventually formed a permanent scar.

D Now the BCG vaccine is only given to infants who are living in regions where the rate of TB is greater than 40 cases in 100 000 people or to infants who are in close contact with the disease. These infants are at a higher risk.

E Although TB is relatively rare in the UK, it is more common in parts of Eastern Europe.

F This is partly due to sufferers not completing the course of antibiotics when they are diagnosed with the disease. The antibiotics have to be taken over a period of six months.

G Some people want to have the BCG vaccine, regardless of its efficacy to protect against the disease.

H Doctors say that if too many people have the disease, then the BCG vaccine will be ineffective. This is because new strains will emerge.

(a) (i) Which **two** paragraphs give reasons why the vaccine BCG is **not** given to all children in the UK now? Write the letters of the two paragraphs. [1]

.... and ....

Keeping Healthy B2

(ii) Which paragraph, **A, B, C, D, E, F, G** or **H**, gives the reasons why certain children still receive the vaccine in parts of the UK? [1]

(iii) Which paragraph, **A, B, C, D, E, F, G** or **H**, explains why it is believed that TB is more common in Eastern Europe? [1]

(iv) If the population of London is 8 000 000 and the rate of TB cases is 40 in 100 000, how many people could be expected to have TB? Show your working. [2]

(b) Why will new strains of TB emerge if too many people catch the disease? [1]

(c) On the axes provided, draw the graph that you would expect to see if a patient with TB **completed** their course of antibiotics. The dashed line on the graph represents the number of harmful bacteria in the body at the start of the treatment. [1]

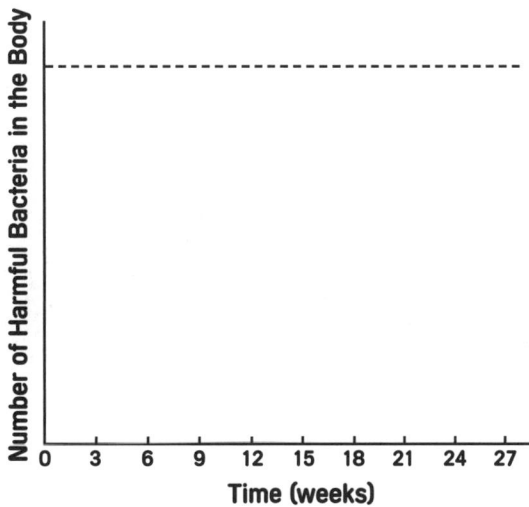

The Effect of Antibiotics on Infection

7. **(a)** What is the **ethical** reason why doctors may not give a placebo to a patient as part of a medical trial? [1]

B2 Keeping Healthy

(b) When might it be difficult to hide whether a patient was on a placebo or not? [1]

....

....

8. Brian is suffering from coronary heart disease. Nobody in his family has died of a heart attack in the past.

(a) What are the most likely reasons for Brian's disease? Put ticks (✓) in the boxes next to the **two** best statements. [2]

He regularly gets stressed at work. ☐   He is vegetarian. ☐

He must carry the genes for heart disease. ☐   He regularly smokes. ☐

(b) Zara is another patient at the same clinic that Brian attends. There have been a large number of patients with heart disease from the part of the country where Zara lives.

What type of study should doctors carry out to find out the cause? Put a ring around the correct answer. [1]

      epidural   **ecclesiastical**   **academic**   **epidemiological**

9. To keep reptiles, such as a bearded dragon, a special habitat has to be set up for them to live in. This is called a vivarium. The diagram shows a vivarium.

Heat lamp ☐

Thermometer ☐

Thermostat ☐

(a) (i) Write **R** in the box next to the part of the vivarium which is a **receptor**. [1]

(ii) Write **E** in the box next to the part of the vivarium which is an **effector**. [1]

(iii) Write **P** in the box next to the part of the vivarium which is a **processor**. [1]

Keeping Healthy — B2

(b) Explain what is meant by **homeostasis**. [1]

....

....

(c) If a mammal was placed in the vivarium, instead of a lizard, what external input would no longer need to be controlled? [1]

....

(d) Which of the following statements best describes homeostasis in lizards? Put a tick (✓) in the box next to the best statement. [1]

It is impossible for lizards to control their body temperature. ☐

Lizards are cold-blooded. ☐

Lizards have to use the environment to keep their bodies warm. ☐

Lizards are mammals. ☐

10. (a) The amount of water that has to be reabsorbed in the body depends on a number of factors. For each of the factors below, decide if a high amount of the factor will lead to concentrated or dilute urine and put ticks (✓) in the correct boxes. The first one has been done for you. [4]

Factor	Urine is concentrated	Urine is dilute
High amount of fluid drunk	☐	✓
High amount of exercise done	☐	☐
High external temperature	☐	☐
High amount of alcohol drunk	☐	☐
High amount of the drug Ecstasy taken	☐	☐

(b) Where in the body is water reabsorbed from the blood? [1]

....

B2 Keeping Healthy

11. Look at the charts for each patient, then answer the questions that follow.

Kathy	**Birendra**	**Jason**	**Mary**
Female	Male	Male	Female
Age 48	Age 50	Age 19	Age 39
Height 165cm	Height 180cm	Height 177cm	Height 158cm
BMI 24	BMI 36	BMI 16	BMI 29
Blood pressure 119/70	Blood pressure 149/90	Blood pressure 100/50	Blood pressure 135/89

(a) What are the risks of each person having a heart attack? Explain your reasons.

The quality of written communication will be assessed in your answer to this question. [6]

(b) What symptoms might Jason be suffering from? Assuming he is not suffering from a disease, what advice would you give to Jason? [3]

(c) What piece of equipment is used for measuring blood pressure? [1]

[Total: .... / 68]

Keeping Healthy — B2

Higher Tier

12. Bacteria grow exponentially. An equation that can be used for the calculation of exponential growth is shown below.

$$x = a \times 2^n$$

This equation enables biologists to calculate the number of bacteria (x) after the population has doubled a given number of times. a = the number of bacteria at the start; n = the number of times the population has doubled.

(a) There are five spores of *Listeria monocytogenes*, a bacterium that causes the deadly disease listeriosis, on a supermarket sandwich. Assuming all the spores start to grow at the same time with a doubling time of 20 minutes, what will the **maximum** number of bacteria be after 24 hours? Show your working. [3]

(b) In practice, numbers of bacteria such as the one you calculated in part **(a)** will never be reached. Suggest why. [2]

B2 Keeping Healthy

13. Read the following report and then answer the questions.

> TeGenero was a company that specialised in creating new drugs. TBN1412 was a drug that was intended to help patients suffering from B-Cell Leukaemia (a disease where memory cells are prevented from making antibodies).
>
> The testing of TBN1412 followed government guidelines. The drug, which was expected to do its job well, had been tested on animals before being tested on humans. For the first human trial, eight male volunteers were involved. Two of the volunteers were given a placebo and the other six were given a dose of TBN1412 that was 500 times lower than that given to the animals. Neither the trial males nor the doctors administering TBN1412 knew whether the trial males were receiving a placebo or the drug itself.
>
> After 5 minutes, six of the eight men started complaining of headaches and pain. Shortly after that, the men started reporting that they felt like they were on fire. All six of the males who received the drug had to be admitted to intensive care.
>
> The drug caused a 'cytokine storm', which is a potentially fatal immune reaction. Cytokines are released by white blood cells to attract other cells to destroy the invader. Unfortunately, with TBN1412 a cytokine storm was triggered and cells started attacking all parts of the immune system. The reaction was completely unanticipated. None of the animals that were tested had any adverse reaction.
>
> The drug trial was reported in the media as being a failure and referred to as a 'drug trial gone wrong'.

(a) What is the name of the type of trial the eight men were involved in? [1]

(b) The British press had headlines stating that the trial was a failure. Explain why the trial was seen as having failed and suggest reasons why it could be regarded as having succeeded.

✎ *The quality of written communication will be assessed in your answer to this question.* [6]

Keeping Healthy B2

(c) It is now thought that the reason why TBN1412 did not show adverse effects in the animals tested was because the drug targeted memory cells and the animals, unusually, did not have any memory cells when they should have had them. The animals that had been tested were monkeys, which have the same immune system as humans. They were only different to wild monkeys in that they were bred and raised in laboratory conditions.

What is the most likely reason why the monkeys did not have memory cells? Put a tick (✓) in the box next to the correct answer. [1]

The monkeys had been genetically engineered, so they did not have memory cells. ☐

Monkeys are not related to us, so do not have the same immune system. ☐

As they were raised in sterile conditions, the monkeys had not been exposed to disease. ☐

The monkeys' memory cells must have come into contact with TBN1412 in the past. ☐

(d) The monkeys' dose had to be scaled down for the humans. If the dose given to the monkeys was 1.2mg, what would the dose in the human volunteers have been? [2]

....

....

14. The table shows how the body loses water. An adult loses 3000cm³ of water in one day.

(a) Complete the table to show the volume of water lost through each method. [4]

How Water is Lost	Percentage	Volume of Water Lost Each Day (cm³)
Urine	40	
Faeces	5	
Sweat	45	
Breathing	10	

(b) (i) What is the name of the hormone that controls the concentration of urine? [1]

....

(ii) What happens to the production of this hormone when alcohol is consumed? [1]

....

(iii) What happens to the production of this hormone when the drug Ecstasy is consumed? [1]

....

[Total: .... / 22]

B3 Life on Earth

1. Zebras and donkeys are members of different species. Zebras can mate with donkeys to produce offspring called zonkeys.

   (a) Which of the following Venn diagrams **best** illustrates the relationship between zebras, donkeys and zonkeys? Put a tick (✓) in the box next to the best diagram. [1]

   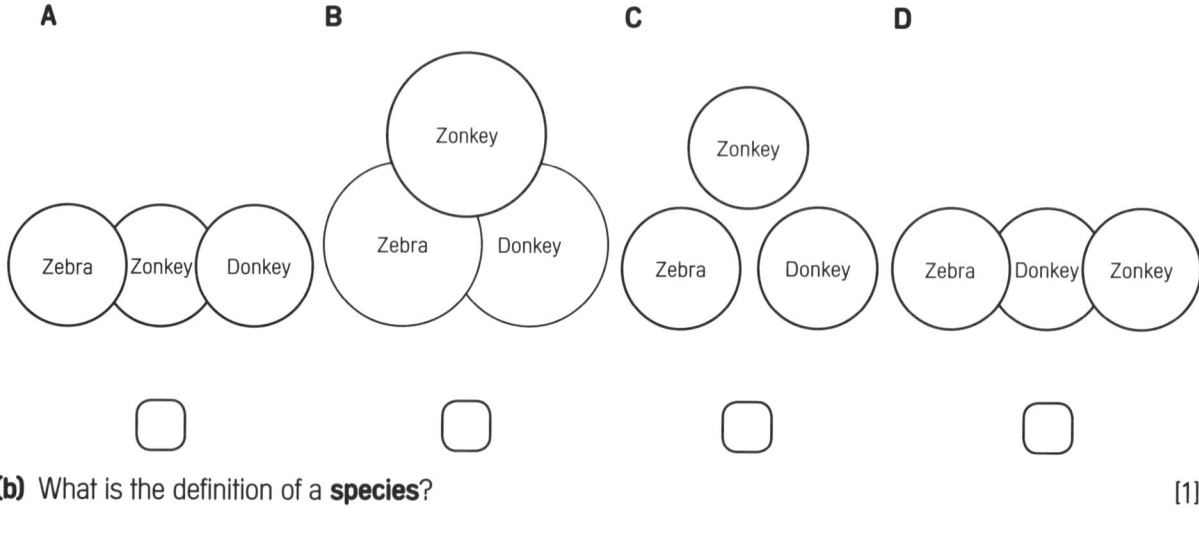

   (b) What is the definition of a **species**? [1]

2. The diagram shows a food web.

   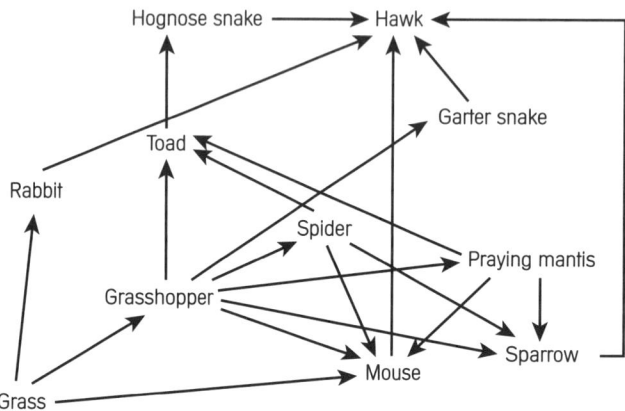

   A disease has reduced the mouse population to very low numbers.

   (a) What feeds on praying mantises? [1]

Life on Earth — B3

(b) Predict what will happen to the grasshopper population. Explain your answer. [1]

(c) Predict what will happen to the rabbit population. Explain your answer. [1]

3. The following information describes the feeding relationship between organisms in a pond.

Water beetles eat mayfly nymphs.

Mayfly nymphs feed on algae.

Water beetles are eaten by sticklebacks.

(a) Draw a **food chain** to illustrate this information. [2]

(b) Which organism is the **autotroph** in this food chain? [1]

(c) Which herbivore is a **heterotroph** in this food chain? [1]

B3 Life on Earth

(d) How many trophic levels are in this food chain? [1]

(e) Give **two** ways in which energy is **lost** from this food chain. [2]

1.

2.

(f) What type of organism breaks down other organisms after they die? [1]

4. **(a)** The diagram shows the carbon cycle. Name the processes **1** to **6** by completing the key below. [4]

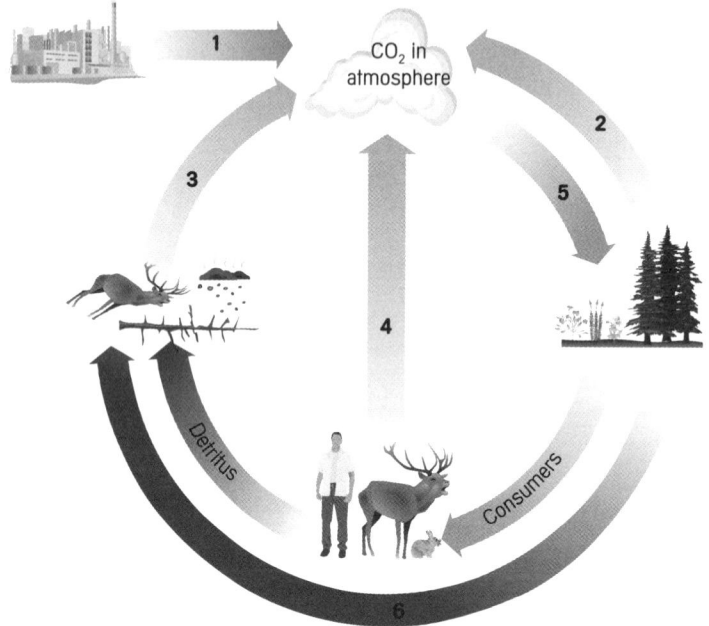

1.

2.

3.

4.

5.

6.

(b) Why is life on Earth said to be carbon-based? [1]

Life on Earth B3

5. The number of fish in the River Lonsdale has been decreasing. Scientists have been called in to find out why.

   (a) The scientists first measure nitrate levels using a dip stick. These are the results:

   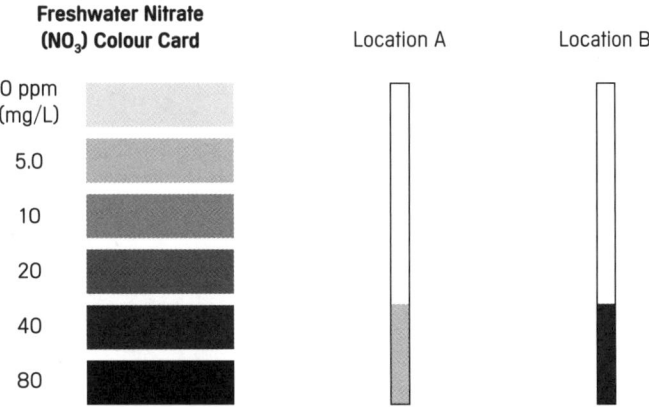

   How much nitrate is present at each of the locations tested? [1]

   Location A: .... ppm   Location B: .... ppm

   (b) The following organisms were found at location A: mayfly nymph, trout, stonefly nymphs.

   The following organisms were found at location B: bloodworms, rat-tailed maggots.

   Explain why the organisms are different at the two locations and suggest why using living organisms is useful.

   ✐ *The quality of written communication will be assessed in your answer to this question.* [6]

6. (a) Scientists study how long ago life started on the Earth and how it evolved. Put a ring around the correct options in these sentences. [3]

   Life is thought to have evolved **2500 / 3500 / 4500** million years ago. One piece of evidence

   for this is from **radiological dating / the Bible / eye witness testimony**. There is evidence that

   fewer / the same number of / many other species previously existed compared with today.

B3 Life on Earth

(b) A group of students is discussing evolution.

Becky
All life on Earth shares a common ancestor. You just need to look at the fossil record and the shared genes that organisms have.

Naveen
Evolution by natural selection is a fact.

Christine
Life on Earth came from a comet that landed on the Earth.

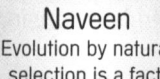

Alan
God put all animals and plants on the Earth. It is clearly written in the Bible.

(i) Who is making a religious argument? [1]

(ii) Who is referring to scientific evidence? [1]

7. In 2010, scientists discovered fossil remains that they believed were a new cousin of modern humans, nicknamed 'Denisovians'. They are thought to have cross-bred with humans. Other scientists were not so sure. They thought that the skeletal remains were just a type of Neanderthal.

Which of the following **best** describes why scientists could reach a different conclusion given the same evidence? Put a tick (✓) in the box next to the best answer. [1]

Scientists have travelled back in time to see the original species. ☐

There is not enough evidence to reach a firm conclusion. ☐

Scientists always stick to what they believe. ☐

It is more fun when there is controversy. ☐

Life on Earth — B3

8. In 1999, the British Government passed a law intended to prevent products being sold with excess packaging. In 2010, the law was used to take a large supermarket to court, as it was selling fresh beef with too much packaging.

(a) Packaging is a problem because it ends up being thrown away. Where does the packaging typically end up? [1]

(b) Even if the packaging is biodegradable, it is still a problem as it decomposes slowly when there is not enough oxygen. Suggest why the packaging decomposes slowly at a landfill site compared with elsewhere. [1]

(c) What **three** things do manufacturers have to consider when designing packaging that will have a minimal effect on the environment? [3]

1.
2.
3.

(d) The case against the supermarket was the first of its kind in the UK. Packaging costs the supermarket money. Suggest one reason why the supermarket sold the beef with excess packaging, assuming that the contents were adequately protected. [1]

(e) What does the term **sustainability** mean? [1]

B3 Life on Earth

9. The diagram shows the energy flow through a food chain.

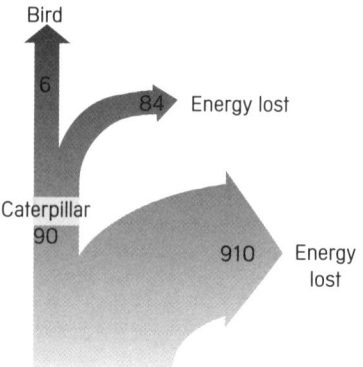

(a) Calculate the percentage of the energy successfully transferred to the caterpillar feeding on the plant. Show your working. [2]

(b) Explain where the energy goes at each stage and suggest why scientists are interested in understanding this.

✎ *The quality of written communication will be assessed in your answer to this question.* [6]

[Total: .... / 46]

Life on Earth B3

Higher Tier

10. At Whitley Wood in the New Forest, biologists discovered that a British species of earthworm was being outcompeted by an invading species which is common in southern Europe. The table below shows data gathered from the wood.

No. of British Earthworms in 1990	100 per m^3
No. of British Earthworms in 2010	10 per m^3

The biologists say that this **proves** that global warming is affecting the climate in the UK. Other scientists disagree. They argue that the data is not reliable enough. Why do they say it is not reliable? Put a tick (✓) in the box next to the **best** answer. [1]

The biologists should not have used earthworms; humans would have been better. ☐

The biologists did not use a satellite to track the temperature changes. ☐

The biologists did not record the colour of the earthworms. ☐

The biologists did not look at other similar locations in the UK to see if the worms were affected in the same way. ☐

11. Biological material will decay over time. There are a variety of organisms that carry out decay. Draw straight lines to show whether each organism is a decomposer or a detritivore. [2]

Organism   **Type**

Earthworm

Bacteria   Decomposer

Woodlouse

                        Detritivore

Fungus

12. Nitrogen is a vital element for survival. Even though 79% of the atmosphere is nitrogen gas, animals cannot use any of it.

    (a) State the **two** ways that nitrogen is fixed into a form useable by animals and plants. [2]

    1. ....

    2. ....

B3 Life on Earth

(b) The diagram shows the nitrogen cycle.

Write the correct number, **1**, **2**, **3** or **4**, in each box. [3]

Eaten by animals ☐

Denitrifying bacteria ☐

Nitrifying bacteria ☐

Nitrogen-fixing bacteria ☐

13. Give the names of **three** processes, other than reproduction, that, when combined, can lead to the formation of a new species. [3]

1. ....
2. ....
3. ....

14. Read the newspaper article.

Evolution Proved?

In 1988, Richard Lenski started a simple experiment that many now believe has proved evolution.

Lenski set up 12 identical flasks containing the bacterium *Escherichia coli (E. coli)* and, every day, 1% of the contents of each flask was subcultured into new flasks of fresh growth media.

Every 500 generations Lenski preserved samples from each population. He stored the samples on agar plates and put them in cold storage. This was equivalent to being a fossil record of the experiment.

In 2010, the 50 000 generation milestone was reached.

After approximately 33 000 generations, bacteria in one flask were suddenly able to consume citrate, a molecule that *E. coli* had never previously been able to use as an energy source.

Life on Earth — B3

(a) Why is storing samples every 500 generations like creating a fossil record? [1]

(b) In what ways is this process **not** like the fossil record? [2]

(c) What must have happened to the DNA of the *E. coli* in the flask where they were able to utilise citrate as an energy source? [1]

(d) Some anti-evolutionists argue that evolution is really just selective breeding. Explain what selective breeding is and argue why this is **not** the case with Lenski's experiment and why his experiment is evidence for evolution.

✎ *The quality of written communication will be assessed in your answer to this question.* [6]

(e) What could a scientist do to prove whether or not the citrate-consuming *E. coli* were the result of a random mutation? Put ticks (✓) in the boxes next to the **two best** statements. [2]

Repeat the experiment. ☐

Go back to an earlier generation and see if the same mutation occurs again. ☐

Use technology to see how the DNA has changed. ☐

Splice the genes and add to a virus vector. ☐

[Total: .... / 23]

B4 The Processes of Life

1. The diagram shows an animal cell.

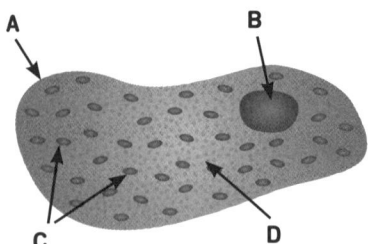

   Which feature of the cell, **A, B, C** or **D**, contains DNA? [1]

   ....

2. All living cells produce enzymes. What type of substance is an enzyme made of? Put a ring around the correct answer. [1]

   carbohydrate**cholesterol****protein****fat**

3. Chloe carried out an investigation to look at the effect of temperature on the action of amylase enzyme on starch. Amylase breaks down starch to sugar.

   Iodine solution is blue-black if starch is present and red-brown if no starch is present.

   Here is Chloe's results table:

Temperature of Starch and Amylase (°C)	Time Taken to Lose Blue-Black Colour (minutes)
20	24
30	11
40	6
60	37
80	Stayed blue-black all the time

   (a) Explain the result for 80°C. [2]

   ....

   ....

   ....

   (b) Chloe kept everything she used and did the same each time, except for changing the temperature. Explain why she did this. [1]

   ....

   ....

The Processes of Life B4

(c) Chloe decided to investigate the effect of temperature with a different enzyme (pepsin), which breaks down protein. Describe a suitable method for evaluating the effect of temperature on pepsin and explain why she would not be able to use starch to indicate enzyme action.

✎ *The quality of written communication will be assessed in your answer to this question.* [6]

4. All living things respire. Explain the roles of cytoplasm and mitochondria in this process and explain how the energy released in this process may be used by the cells of the organism.

✎ *The quality of written communication will be assessed in your answer to this question.* [6]

5. Plants use photosynthesis to produce glucose.

(a) Complete the word equation for this process. [2]

.... + Water ⟶ Glucose + ...

(b) Sunlight provides the energy for this reaction.

What is the name of the green pigment that absorbs this energy? [1]

(c) If a plant is grown in poor light, how will its growth be affected? [1]

B4 The Processes of Life

6. Damien wanted to investigate the number of buttercups in a field near his house. The edge of the field is lined with trees. Damien took three transects, starting by the field edge, walking away from the trees towards the middle of the field. Every two metres he placed his 1m² quadrat on the ground and counted the number of buttercups in each one.

He plotted the average number of buttercups in each quadrat in his three transects on a graph.

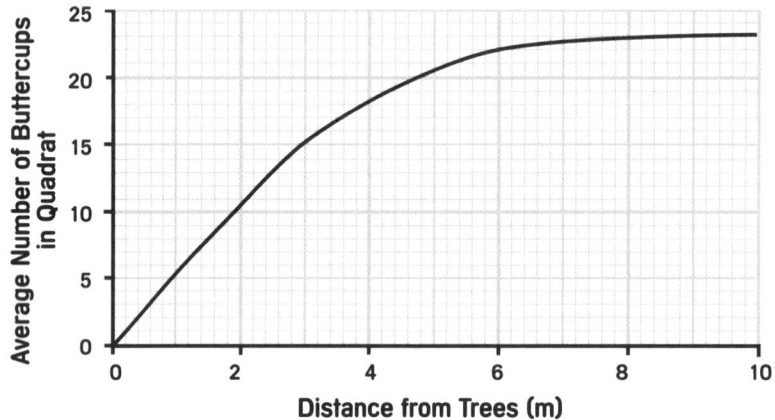

(a) On average, how many buttercups did Damien find four metres from the trees? [1]

(b) Describe the pattern shown by the graph. [2]

(c) Why did Damien use the mean of three transects? [1]

7. Petra thought that light would affect the growth of a seedling. She took four identical, well-watered seedlings in pots and placed one seedling (A) in a warm cupboard. She placed another seedling (B) in a refrigerated cupboard (by accident). She placed seedling C on a warm, sunny windowsill for most of the day and seedling D on a windowsill that was in shade most of the day.

After a week she found the following:

- Seedling A had grown tall, but was very thin and yellow.
- Seedling B showed no change at all.
- Seedling C was taller and looking very healthy.
- Seedling D was healthy-looking but had only grown a little bit.

Petra concluded that it was not light which affected the growth of the seedlings, but that it was the temperature which caused the effects. Evaluate Petra's conclusion, considering her evidence. Give reasons to explain your answer.

The Processes of Life B4

✏️ *The quality of written communication will be assessed in your answer to this question.* [6]

_____

_____

_____

_____

_____

_____

_____

8. Energy for cell processes is released by respiration.

  (a) Most animal cells respire aerobically. What is the word equation for aerobic respiration? [2]

  _____

  (b) Muscle cells in the arms and legs are able to respire anaerobically. Give **two** ways in which anaerobic respiration here differs from aerobic respiration. [2]

  1. _____

  2. _____

  (c) Energy from respiration is used for many processes in cells.

   (i) What is the name of the type of protein that uses energy from respiration in plant cells to synthesise starch and cellulose? [1]

   _____

   (ii) What is the name of the chemicals made from glucose and nitrates using energy from respiration in plant, animal and microbial cells? [1]

   _____

9. The diagram shows a plant cell.

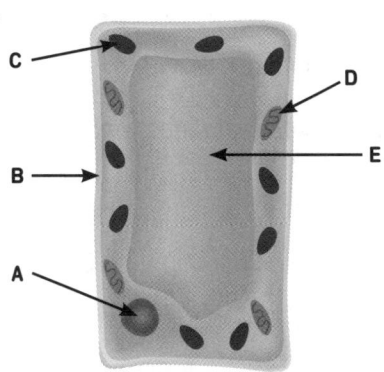

Not to scale

B4 The Processes of Life

(a) Write the correct letter, **A**, **B**, **C**, **D** or **E**, in each box.

(i) Allows only certain substances to enter or leave the cell ☐ [1]

(ii) Contains the genetic code for enzymes used in photosynthesis ☐ [1]

(iii) Used by the cell to store waste materials and to regulate water levels ☐ [1]

(b) Bacterial cells have different structures from animal cells. Give **two** ways in which they differ. [2]

1. ....

2. ....

10. Susie made some jellies for a party. She put some fresh pineapple in them but did not have quite enough, so for some of the jellies she used tinned pineapple. She noticed that the jellies with the tinned pineapple set a long while before the jellies with the fresh pineapple.

She carried out the following investigation to find out what happened.

In a test tube, labelled A, she put a 5g cube of jelly and added 15cm³ of water.

In a second test tube, labelled B, she put a 5g cube of jelly and added 15cm³ of fresh pineapple juice.

In a third test tube, labelled C, she put a 5g cube of jelly and added 15cm³ of boiled and cooled pineapple juice (to represent the cooking during the tinning process).

Her results are given in the table.

Test Tube	A	B	C
Result	No change after 2 hours	Jelly disappeared after 1 hour	No change after 2 hours

(a) What conclusion could Susie suggest from this result? [1]

....

....

(b) What was the purpose of tube A? [1]

....

(c) Jelly is made of a protein called gelatine.

(i) What name is given to substances that digest proteins? [1]

....

(ii) What did boiling the pineapple juice used in tube C do to this substance? [1]

....

The Processes of Life B4

(d) What would Susie's results have been like if she had used 5g of chopped up jelly instead of a 5g cube? Give a reason for your answer. [2]

11. Biogas is a fuel made from the waste products of living things. It is made by allowing bacteria to ferment waste material such as cattle dung, human faeces and vegetable waste.

   (a) Suggest why 'biogas' is given this name. [1]

   (b) The biogas generator is airtight. Why is this important for it to work efficiently? [1]

   (c) Generators produce two gases. One is carbon dioxide. What is the other? [1]

   (d) Suggest **two** environmental advantages of burning biogas. [2]

   1.

   2.

12. Yeast can respire with or without oxygen.

   (a) In bread making, yeast is used to make the dough rise and give the bread a fluffy texture. What is the name of the gas produced by yeast that does this? [1]

   (b) In brewing, if air is allowed into the fermenter, alcohol is not produced by the respiration of yeast. Explain why. [2]

   (c) In both baking and brewing, sugar needs to be present or added. Why is sugar necessary? [1]

B4 The Processes of Life

13. A group of friends is discussing photosynthesis after a lesson.

Jack: Photosynthesis needs heat energy from the Sun.

Emily: Photosynthesis needs light energy from the Sun.

Darren: Chlorophyll absorbs the energy from the Sun.

Paul: The sugar made is stored as protein in the roots.

Grace: Photosynthesis needs oxygen to make the sugar.

Which **two** people are making correct statements? [2]

_____ and _____

14. The diagram shows a variegated leaf. When exposed to light in normal growing conditions, the outer margin of the leaf is white and the inner part of the leaf is green.

The Processes of Life — B4

(a) Students wanted to find out if both the green and the white areas of the leaf produced starch. Before the plant from which this leaf was taken was used in the experiment, it was watered and placed in the dark for 48 hours. Explain why this was done. [2]

(b) The plant was then placed in a light position for 48 hours. The leaf shown was removed from the plant and tested for starch. Where would you expect starch to be present? Give a reason for your answer. [2]

15. In the past, gardeners used to burn wood inside a greenhouse to encourage their plants to grow faster. Explain why burning wood could cause plants to grow faster, but could also potentially slow plant growth. Use information from the graph in your answer, along with your own knowledge of how light can be a limiting factor.

Effect of Carbon Dioxide Concentration and Temperature on the Rate of Photosynthesis

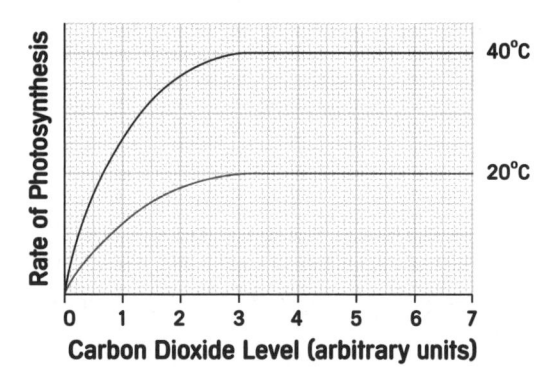

Rate of Photosynthesis vs *Carbon Dioxide Level (arbitrary units)* — curves shown for 40°C and 20°C.

✎ The quality of written communication will be assessed in your answer to this question. [6]

[Total: .... / 69]

B4 The Processes of Life

Higher Tier

16. Plants use photosynthesis to produce glucose.

Complete the balanced symbol equation for this process. [2]

$$\_\_\_\_ + 6H_2O \longrightarrow C_6H_{12}O_6 + \_\_\_\_$$

17. Aamad carried out an investigation to look at the effect of pH on the action of the enzyme pepsin on egg white, a protein, which looks cloudy in a test tube. Pepsin breaks down protein.

Aamad's results are shown in the table.

pH of Egg White and Pepsin	Time Taken to Clear (minutes)
1	4
4	11
7	39
9	Stayed cloudy
11	Stayed cloudy

(a) The optimum pH for pepsin is pH 1. Aamad says his results support that statement. Do you agree? Explain your answer. [1]

(b) Aamad expected this pattern of results due to his knowledge of the lock-and-key hypothesis. Explain the lock-and-key hypothesis and describe how denaturing affects enzymes for both temperature and pH. Suggest why the optimum pH for pepsin in humans is pH 1.

The quality of written communication will be assessed in your answer to this question. [6]

The Processes of Life — B4

18. The diagram shows a root hair cell.

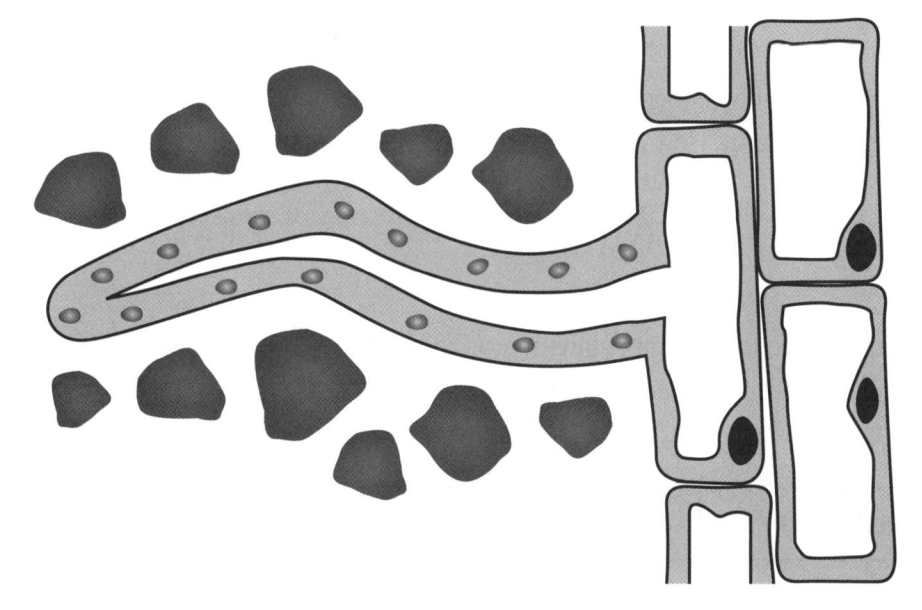

(a) What is the name of the process by which soil water moves into the root hair cell? [1]

....

(b) What is the name of the process by which mineral salts, such as nitrates, are absorbed into the root hair cell? [1]

....

(c) There are a large number of mitochondria in this cell. Why are these necessary for the absorption of nitrates? [1]

....

....

19. Which of the following statements best explains the term **osmosis**? Put a tick (✓) in the box next to the best answer. [1]

The movement of a substance against a concentration gradient ☐

The movement of solutes from low to high concentration ☐

The movement of water from a concentrated solution to a less concentrated solution ☐

The movement of water from a dilute solution to a more concentrated solution ☐

B4 The Processes of Life

20. (a) Write a balanced symbol equation for aerobic respiration. [3]

(b) Rice is planted in waterlogged and therefore oxygen-deficient conditions, but its roots can still produce energy. How can it respire in such conditions? [1]

21. In an experiment to investigate osmosis, cylinders were cut from a large potato, blotted dry and weighed. They were then placed in different solutions of salt water. After 30 minutes they were removed from the solutions, blotted dry and reweighed. The results are shown in the table.

Salt Solution (M)	0.0	0.2	0.4	0.6	0.8
Mass at Start (g)	1.2	1.2	1.2	1.2	1.2
Mass at End (g)	1.4	1.2	1.1	1.0	0.8

(a) Why did the potato in the 0.0M solution gain mass? [2]

(b) Why did the potato in the 0.8M solution lose mass? [2]

[Total: .... / 21]

Growth and Development — B5

1. Draw straight lines to join the words to their correct descriptions. [3]

   Word

   - Egg
   - Fertilisation
   - Sperm

   Description

   - The fusion of a male gamete with a female gamete
   - The division of the fertilised nucleus
   - A male gamete
   - A female gamete

2. (a) What is the name of the process by which the cells in a zygote divide? [1]

   ....

   (b) Why is it important that gametes only have half the number of chromosomes as the parent cell? [1]

   ....

   ....

3. Stem cells can be used to produce any type of specialised cell required.

   (a) What is the difference between embryonic stem cells and adult stem cells? [2]

   ....

   ....

   (b) What is the best stage of development to take embryonic stem cells? Put a ring around the correct answer. [1]

       8 cell stage   16 cell stage   32 cell stage   64 cell stage

   (c) Why can't cells that come from an embryo at any stage be used as embryonic stem cells? [1]

   ....

4. A salivary gland cell has the same genes as all other cells in the body. Which of the following genes would you expect to be active in the salivary gland? Put ticks (✓) in the boxes next to the **two** correct answers. [2]

   - Eye colour ☐
   - Salivary amylase production ☐
   - ADH production ☐
   - Membrane protein formation ☐

B5 Growth and Development

5. **(a)** How can stem cells be used to help in medicine? [1]

(b) People suffering from diseases such as leukaemia often have chemotherapy, which damages bone marrow. Bone marrow transplants replace the patients' bone marrow, enabling new blood cells to be made. What must be in the bone marrow for new cells to be created? [1]

6. **(a)** What is the name of the process by which plant cells in the growing shoot tip divide? Put a ring around the correct answer. [1]

        meiosis   **fertilisation**   **mitosis**   **cloning**

(b) Give **two** differences between growth in plants and growth in animals. [2]

1.

2.

7. Marie carried out an investigation into the effect of light on maize shoots. She set up four plants, **A**, **B**, **C** and **D**, which are described below.

A	Shoot tip cut off and covered; given all-round sunlight
B	Shoot given sunlight from the left.
C	Shoot given sunlight from the right.
D	Shoot given all-round sunlight.

After three days, Marie's results were as follows:

A	Did not grow.
B	Grew and bent to the left.
C	Grew and bent to the right.
D	Grew straight up.

(a) Marie realised that the maize was responding to the light. Explain why the response of maize would increase its chance of survival. [2]

Growth and Development B5

(b) Which maize shoot was the control in the experiment? [1]

(c) What was the **independent** variable in this experiment? [1]

8. Some of the stages of the human life cycle are shown in this diagram.

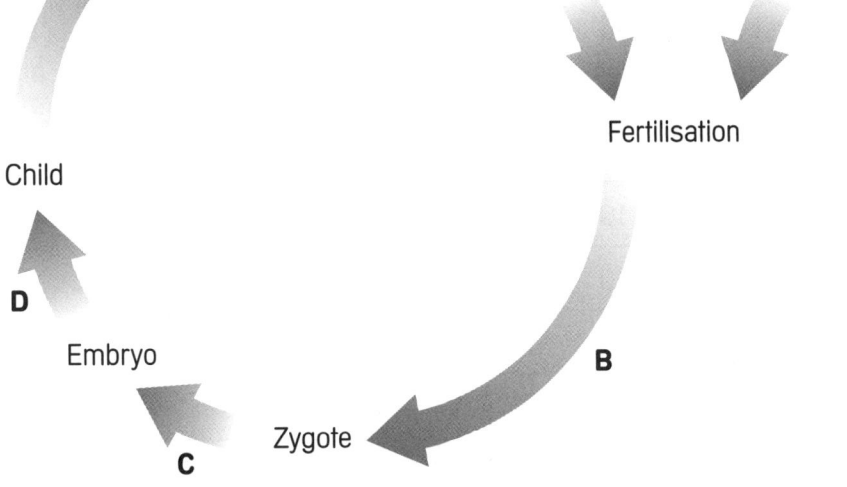

(a) At which stage, **A**, **B**, **C** or **D**, does meiosis occur? [1]

(b) Human body cells have a chromosome number of 46. If one of these cells divides by meiosis, what is the chromosome number in each of the cells produced? Put a ring around the correct answer.

        23   **46**   **69**   **92** [1]

9. Describe the main processes involved in the cell cycle from a single adult cell to new genetically identical cells in an embryo. [3]

B5 Growth and Development

10. The genetic code is carried within the structure of DNA. Complete the following sentences about DNA. Use words from this list. [4]

base   gene   single   double   triple
carbohydrate   protein   fat

The DNA molecule has a _____ helix structure. The strands of the DNA have four

different kinds of _____. The order of these in a _____ is the

genetic code for the production of a _____.

11. Carrie was doing an experiment looking at the growth of microbes in a liquid broth. The broth contained all the nutrients needed for the microbes to grow and it went cloudy as the population of microbes increased. She incubated the tubes of broth at a range of temperatures for 48 hours and recorded her observations. Here is her table of results:

Temperature (°C)	Appearance after 48 hours
10	Clear
20	Slightly cloudy
30	Cloudy
40	Very cloudy
50	Slightly cloudy
60	Clear

Carrie had predicted that the higher the temperature, the more the microbe would grow.

(a) When Carrie set up the tubes, she made sure that each one was prepared in exactly the same way and that all conditions other than temperature were the same. Explain why this was necessary. [2]

(b) Carrie's observations did not quite match her prediction. What evidence is there to support her prediction? [1]

Growth and Development B5

(c) Carrie concluded that microbes stopped growing at 50°C. Was she correct in that statement? Use the evidence in the table to support your answer. [1]

(d) Her friend, Raj, did the same experiment, but he shone a light through the broth and used a light sensor to obtain a reading of how much light passed through. Raj said he wanted to be more precise than Carrie. Do you agree that he was more precise? Give a reason for your answer. [1]

12. When plants grow, cells divide to make new ones in certain regions of the plant.

(a) What is the name of the process of cell division in these regions? [1]

(b) What name is given to these regions of the plant? [1]

(c) The new cells formed in these regions are unspecialised. What does **unspecialised** mean? [1]

(d) If a tip of a plant containing these regions is cut off, it can be used to clone the plant as a cutting. Why is this only possible using these regions? [2]

B5 Growth and Development

13. The diagrams show two plants. Plant A was grown in good light in a warm place and watered well. Plant B was grown in the dark in a warm place and watered well, but was laid on its side. When they were initially planted, both plants were identical.

A

B

Explain why plant B has grown the way it has. [2]

....

....

....

14. When two gametes fuse together at fertilisation, they form a new cell which will divide and develop into a new organism.

(a) What is the name of the single cell formed at fertilisation? [1]

....

(b) What type of cell division produces gametes? [1]

....

(c) The cell formed at fertilisation then divides into two cells. What type of cell division is this? [1]

....

(d) At first these new cells are unspecialised. What are these cells called? [1]

....

15. The diagrams represent two types of cell division.

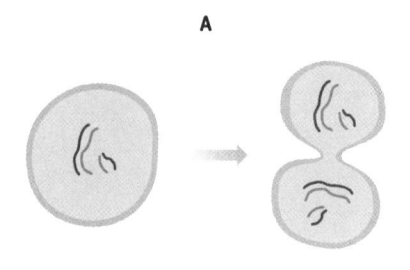

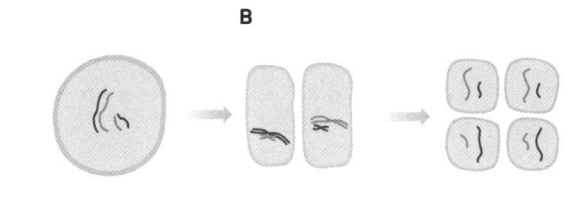

A

B

OCR Twenty First Century GCSE Biology A Workbook Answers

Answering Quality of Written Communication Questions

A number of the questions in your examinations will include an assessment of the quality of your written communication (QWC). These questions are worth a maximum of 6 marks and are indicated by a pencil icon (✏).

Your answers to these questions will be marked according to...
- the level of your understanding of the relevant science
- how well you structure your answer
- the style of your writing, including the quality of your punctuation, grammar and spelling.

QWC questions will be marked using a 'Levels of Response' mark scheme. The examiner will decide whether your answer is in the top level, middle level or bottom level. The expected quality of written communication is different in the three levels and it will always be considered at the same time as looking at the scientific information in your answer:
- To achieve Level 3 (which is the top level and is worth 5–6 marks), your answer should contain relevant science, and be organised and presented in a structured and coherent manner. You should use scientific terms appropriately and your spelling, punctuation and grammar should have very few errors.
- For Level 2 (worth 3–4 marks), there may be more errors in your spelling, punctuation and grammar, and your answer will miss some of the things expected at Level 3.

- For Level 1 (worth 1–2 marks), your answer may be written using simplistic language. You will have included some relevant science, but the quality of your written communication may have limited how well the examiner can understand your answer. This could be due to lots of errors in spelling, punctuation and grammar, misuse of scientific terms or a poor structure.
- An answer given Level 0 may contain insufficient or irrelevant science, and will not be given any marks.

You will be awarded the higher or lower mark within a particular level depending on the quality of the science and the quality of the written communication in your answer.

Even if the quality of your written communication is perfect, the level you are awarded will be limited if you show little understanding of the relevant science, and you will be given Level 0 if you show no relevant scientific understanding at all.

To help you understand the criteria above, three specimen answers are provided to the first QWC question in this workbook. The first is a model answer worth 6 marks, the second answer would be worth 4 marks and the third answer worth 2 marks. The three exemplar answers are differentiated by their scientific content and use of scientific terminology. Model answers worth 6 marks are provided to all other QWC questions to help you aspire to the best possible marks.

Module B1: You and Your Genes (Pages 3–12)

1. (a) There will be a difference in the offspring due to the air quality **should be ticked**.
   (b) **Any one from:** 60% of the offspring stayed awake at night; Only 40% of the offspring slept at night.
   (c) **Any one from:** 0.6 × 250 = 150 offspring; (60 ÷ 100) × 250 = 150 offspring
   [1 for correct working but wrong answer]
   (d) The sample size was too low. Increasing the sample size would improve the reliability of the experiment.
   (e) Thinking creatively **should be ticked**.

2. (a) AA
   (b) Tad: Aa
       Deborah: Aa
   (c) **This is a model answer which would score full marks:**
   As Spencer is a carrier of the SMA allele, he has the dominant allele A and the recessive allele a. Alev has no family history of SMA, so it is likely that she is carrying both dominant alleles. If they were to have children, each child would get at least one dominant allele, so none of the children would have the condition. Testing adults for genetic disorders means that people have a better idea of the chances of their future offspring getting a disorder. However, the tests are not 100% reliable and could lead to couples choosing not to have children when they actually do not carry the disorder.
   This answer would score 4 marks: None of the children would get it as Alev must be AA. This means that every child would definitely get a dominant gene. As the disease is recessive, there is a 100% chance they would not have the disorder. Testing means that the parents would have a better idea of what genetic disorders their child may have.
   This answer would score 2 marks: Spencer has Aa. One of his children might get the disease because they could get the a gene from him but not from Alev, who does not carry it.

3. **Lines should be drawn from** Huntington's **to** Memory loss **and** Mood changes.
   Lines should be drawn from Cystic fibrosis **to** Difficulty digesting food **and** Difficulty breathing.

4. (a) (i) 4 and 5 **[Both needed for 1 mark.]**
       (ii) 5
   (b) 1 in 5 **should be ringed**.

5. (a) Darby
   (b) Gwyneth

6. (a) Although there is a correlation, it does not necessarily mean that there is also a cause **and** As children grow, their feet grow too. In addition, as they grow their brains will develop more **should be ticked**.
   (b)

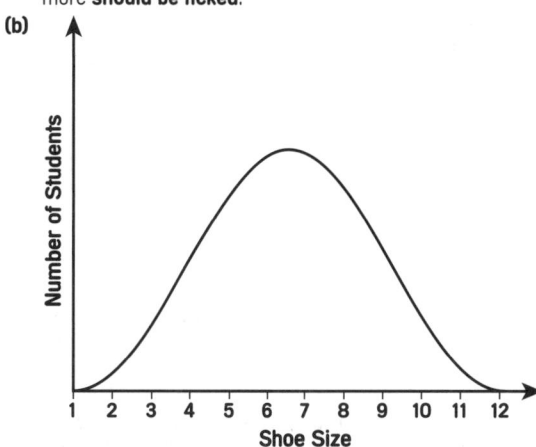

   [Graph showing a normal distribution curve with Shoe Size (1–12) on the x-axis and Number of Students on the y-axis, peaking around shoe size 6–7]

   [1 for a correctly shaped curve; 1 for labelling the y-axis Number of Students / Frequency. Accept a bar chart which shows a normal distribution curve.]

7. (a) One egg was fertilised by one sperm which divided once and then separated, and then each cell divided and separated again **should be ticked**.
    (b) The way their ear lobes are attached will be the same **should be ticked**.
    (c) That in every 64 000 000 successful births **[1]** only one will be of quads **[1]**
    (d) The environment causes subtle differences **should be ticked**.

8. (a) Mm
    (b) Cannot taste MSG
    (c) (i) **Any one from:** 1 in 2; 0.5; $\frac{1}{2}$; 50%
        (ii) **Any one from:** 1 in 4; 0.25; $\frac{1}{4}$; 25%
        (iii) **Any one from:** 1 in 4; 0.25; $\frac{1}{4}$; 25%
    (d) (i) Ratio MM : Mn : mm would be 1 : 2 : 1
        (ii) Ratio able to taste : not able to taste would be 3 : 1

9. Adele has the sex chromosomes XY **and** Adele's body cannot detect the hormone androgen **should be ticked**.

10. **This is a model answer which would score full marks:**
    In vitro fertilisation is undertaken. Each resulting embryo has a single cell removed when it arrives at the 8 cell stage. The single cell is tested to see if the allele for the genetic disorder that is causing concern is present. If it is not, then the embryo is implanted into the mother and the pregnancy continues as normal. If it has the disorder, the embryo is destroyed. The ethical issues are that, rather than allowing a prospective embryo to develop normally, we are choosing which one will have the chance. There is a risk to the embryos that are tested – removing a cell could have an effect in the long term on the development of the child. There is also an argument that the non-implanted embryos should not be destroyed as they too could have developed into a human being.

11. … can only be taken from an embryo up to the 8 cell stage; … have the potential to become any cell type **and** … are unspecialised cells **should be ticked**. **[2 for all correct; 1 for two correct]**

12. (a) April; Skirmante **[Both needed for 1 mark.]**
    (b) Matthew; Jonathan **[Both needed for 1 mark.]**

13. (a) Personalised medicine is where the particular genes that a patient has are taken into account when planning their treatment **[1]**. Some drugs may not work with some people and new technology means a drug can be given only to those that it will work on **[1]**. It also means that side effects should be minimised and the chance that the treatment will be successful should be improved **[1]**.
    (b) If the result is a false positive, then you will not receive a drug which may have helped you **[1]**. If the result is a false negative, then you will be prescribed the drug when it will cause side effects **[1]**.
    (c) **Any one from:** Employers may use the information to not employ you; Insurers may not cover you; The information could fall into the wrong hands.

14. (a) So that it is possible to tell whether the organism is a clone or not
    (b) 1 in 217 eggs / embryos grew
        Percentage efficiency = 1 ÷ 217 × 100
        = 0.46%
        [1 for correct working but wrong answer]
    (c) **This is a model answer which would score full marks:**
        The process of cloning mammals is very inefficient. The success rate with Dolly the sheep was 0.46%, which is very low. If this was repeated with humans, there would be lots of embryos that would die or fail to develop, and a large proportion of the population is against this. People would also argue that too many eggs need to be collected and these could potentially have become human beings. On the other hand, some scientists may want to clone humans to provide supplies of organs, which could be used to save lives. There will also be a small number who want to do it as a challenge, to push the boundaries of science.
    (d) Not all genomes of adult cells can lead to the development of a new organism **should be ticked**.

Module B2: Keeping Healthy
(Pages 13–23)

1. (a) Microorganisms have antibodies on their surface **should be ticked**.
    (b) Other scientists have not been able to check his results **should be ticked**.

2. (a) 1 000 000 × 0.9999 = 999 900;
        1 000 000 − 999 900 = 100
        or 1 000 000 × 0.0001 = 100
        [1 for correct working but wrong answer.]
    (b) 5 hours = 5 × 60 minutes = 300 minutes
        $x(t) = a \times b^{t/\tau}$
        = 100 × $2^{300/30}$
        = 100 × 2^{10}
        = 100 × 1024
        = 102 400 bacteria
        [1 for correct working but wrong answer]
    (c) **Any three from:** Water; Oxygen; Food; Heat

3. (a) (i) (400 000 ÷ 61 000 000) × 100 = 0.66%
            [1 for correct working but wrong answer]
        (ii) (80 ÷ 61 000 000) × 100 = 0.00013%
            [1 for correct working but wrong answer]
        (iii) It enables people to work out the chance of getting food poisoning and the chance of dying from *Campylobacter*, so they can make an informed decision about buying chicken.
    (b) There is a correlation, which only suggests that there may be a cause **and** There are other sources of *Campylobacter* **should be ticked**.
    (c) **This is a model answer which would score full marks:**
        Everything we do carries a risk. The risk with *Campylobacter* is relatively small, with less than 1% of people getting this type of food poisoning and a very small number dying from it. Food poisoning does not only come from meat; it also comes from not washing your hands and not cleaning vegetables. The press sometimes over-emphasise risk or make it seem higher than it actually is by only reporting newsworthy stories. If someone has had food poisoning before, they may be more familiar with the risk and fear it more. Not eating meat also carries a risk – we need the protein and vitamins to grow. In future, Astra washing her hands and work surfaces, as well as cooking meat thoroughly, will minimise the risk.

4. (a) Spencer
    (b) Siobhan
    (c) Salma
    (d) **This is a model answer which would score full marks:**
        Vaccination involves injecting a safe form of the disease-causing microorganism into the body. White blood cells recognise the antigens on the surface of the vaccine. The white blood cells then 'remember' the antigens, so when the real disease is caught, it is killed before it kills the patient. Diseases which have a vaccine against them are either potentially life-threatening or do considerable harm when caught, for example, causing brain damage or making the patient sterile. The side effects of the vaccine are normally not very serious or are much rarer than getting the disease itself. Therefore, the benefit of having the vaccination outweighs the risk of a side effect. If too few people are vaccinated, then there will be a pool of people that the disease could flourish in, eventually mutating and infecting those who were vaccinated previously.

5. chemicals; kill; bacteria; viruses

6. (a) (i) **Any two from:** B; C; E **[Both needed for 1 mark.]**
        (ii) D
        (iii) F

(iv) 40 cases in 100 000
so 40 × 80 = 3200 cases in 8 000 000
[1 for correct working but wrong answer]

(b) The larger the pool of people with the disease, the greater the chance of a bacterium emerging that has mutated into a new strain.

(c) **Any suitable graph which starts at the dashed line and decreases as a curve, ultimately ending at 0 on the y-axis, e.g.**

The Effect of Antibiotics on Infection

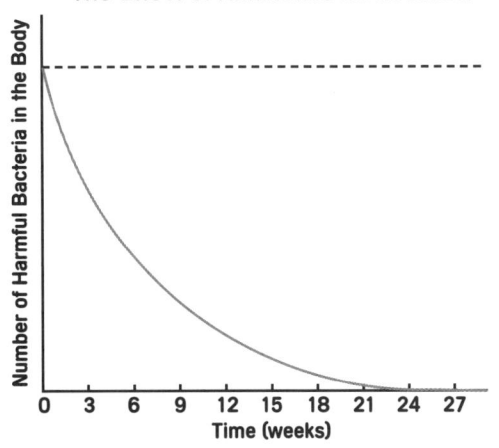

7. (a) It is not right to withhold a medical treatment that could cure someone or make them feel better. A placebo has no effect.
   (b) When the drug causes an obvious effect.

8. (a) He regularly gets stressed at work **and** He regularly smokes **should be ticked**.
   (b) epidemiological **should be ringed**.

9. (a) (i)–(iii)

   Heat lamp — E
   Thermometer — R
   Thermostat — P

   (b) Homeostasis is the maintenance of a constant internal environment.
   (c) Temperature
   (d) Lizards have to use the environment to keep their bodies warm **should be ticked**.

10. (a)

	Urine is concentrated	Urine is dilute
High amount of fluid drunk		✓
High amount of exercise done	✓	
High external temperature	✓	
High amount of alcohol drunk		✓
High amount of the drug Ecstasy taken	✓	

[1 for one correct; 2 for two correct; 3 for three correct; 4 for all four correct]

(b) The kidneys

11. (a) **This is a model answer which would score full marks:**
Birendra is most likely to suffer from a heart attack. This is because his BMI is 36, which is much higher than the highest healthy reading of 25. Birendra's blood pressure is also very high, suggesting there is a lot of pressure in the arteries. High BMI and blood pressure are indicators for a heart attack. Mary is overweight and has an increased chance of having a heart attack. Kathy has a normal BMI, which means her body mass is within the normal range for her height. It is unlikely that she will have a heart attack based on her BMI. Jason's BMI is low. His chance of suffering a heart attack is low, although he may have other health problems.

(b) Jason will probably feel tired and light-headed **[1]**. His BMI suggests that he is underweight **[1]**. He should try to increase the amount of food in his diet **[1]**.

(c) A sphygmomanometer

12. (a) $n = (24h \times 60min) \div 20min$
    $n = 72$ **[1]**
    $x = a \times 2^n$
    $x = 5 \times 2^{72}$
    $x = 2.36 \times 10^{22}$ bacteria
    [1 for second calculation and 1 for correct answer. Allow error in first step carried forward to second half of calculation.]

(b) After a certain number of generations, food, space and other factors become limiting **[1]**. The population will not have enough resources to survive and breed **[1]**.

13. (a) Double blind
    (b) **This is a model answer which would score full marks:**
Drug trials are designed to determine whether a drug works or not. They also show whether there are any side effects. With this particular trial, the drug had already been successfully tested on animals. The effect on humans could not have been predicted. Therefore the trial, although harming the volunteers, did prove that it was not safe to use on humans and so was a success. However, six of the volunteers suffered a violent reaction, had to be admitted to intensive care and nearly lost their lives.

(c) As they were raised in sterile conditions, the monkeys had not been exposed to disease **should be ticked.**

(d) $1.2 \div 500 = 0.0024$mg or 2.4μm
[1 for correct working but wrong answer]

14. (a)

How Water is Lost	Percentage	Volume of Water Lost Each Day (cm³)
Urine	40	1200
Faeces	5	150
Sweat	45	1350
Breathing	10	300

(b) (i) Anti-diuretic hormone / ADH
    (ii) ADH production decreases
    (iii) ADH production increases

Module B3: Life on Earth
(Pages 24–33)

1. (a) **Diagram A should be ticked.**
   (b) The ability to breed and produce fertile offspring.

2. (a) Sparrows, mice and toads **[All three needed for 1 mark.]**
   (b) **Any one from:** The grasshopper population will increase because there are fewer mice to eat them; The grasshopper population will decrease because other organisms that would have fed on the mice now feed on them.
   (c) **Any one from:** The rabbit population will increase because there is more grass for them to eat, owing to fewer mice feeding on it; The rabbit population will decrease because there are fewer mice for hawks to eat, so they will attempt to compensate with other things they eat.

3. (a) Algae ⟶ Mayfly nymphs ⟶ Water beetles ⟶ Sticklebacks
    [1 for correct order; 1 for the arrows pointing in the correct direction]
    (b) Algae
    (c) Mayfly nymphs
    (d) Four
    (e) **Any two from:** Excreted waste; Respiration; Trapped in indigestible material; Movement of organisms
    (f) Decomposers

4. (a) 1 Combustion; 2, 3 and 4 Respiration **[all three needed for 1 mark]**; 5 Photosynthesis; 6 Death
    (b) All organic molecules contain carbon.

5. (a) Location A: 5.0 (ppm); Location B: 40 (ppm) **[Both needed for 1 mark.]**
    (b) **This is a model answer which would score full marks:**
    The evidence suggests that the nitrate levels are much higher at location B than at location A. The nitrate is polluting the river and has changed the conditions. Bloodworms and rat-tailed maggots are pollution-loving organisms. As they are found at location B, it confirms the presence of pollutants. At location A, organisms that can only live in unpolluted water are found. All organisms have different environmental preferences, so their presence or absence can indicate problems in the environment. This is a very quick technique that provides evidence without much disruption to the environment.

6. (a) 3500; radiological dating **and** many other **should be ringed**.
    (b) (i) Alan
        (ii) Becky

7. There is not enough evidence to reach a firm conclusion **should be ticked**.

8. (a) **Any one from:** Landfill sites; Incinerator plants
    (b) Because there is more waste at a landfill using up available oxygen, there is less available for the organisms that would break down the packaging.
    (c) **Any three from:** What materials should be used; How much energy is used; How much pollution will be produced; Time to rot; Release of chemicals; Effect on other organisms
    (d) The packaging is used to attract the customer to get them to buy the product.
    (e) Meeting the needs of people today without damaging the Earth for future generations

9. (a) Percentage of energy successfully transferred
    $= \dfrac{\text{Amount used}}{\text{Amount potentially available}} \times 100$
    $= (90 \div 1000) \times 100$
    $= 9\%$
    [1 for correct working but wrong answer]
    (b) **This is a model answer which would score full marks:**
    A proportion of the energy that comes from the Sun is captured and stored in the plant tissue. The caterpillar eats the plant and some of the energy is transferred. It is either stored in the caterpillar's body or lost through respiration, movement or keeping the caterpillar warm. The bird eats the caterpillar and stores some of the energy in its body. The rest, like in the caterpillar, is lost through respiration, movement or keeping the bird warm. Scientists are interested in this because they can determine the efficiency of a food web and better understand what will happen if parts of the food web are disturbed – for example, if new organisms are introduced or others are removed (by hunting or for food products).

10. The biologists did not look at other similar locations in the UK to see if the worms were affected in the same way **should be ticked**.

11. Lines should be drawn from Earthworm **and** Woodlouse **to** Detritivore. **[Both needed for 1 mark.]**
    Lines should be drawn from Bacteria **and** Fungus **to** Decomposer. **[Both needed for 1 mark.]**

12. (a) Nitrogen-fixing bacteria; Lightning strikes
    (b) Eaten by animals 4; Denitrifying bacteria 1; Nitrifying bacteria 3; Nitrogen-fixing bacteria 2 **[1 for each correct answer up to a maximum of 3.]**

13. **Any three from:** Mutations; Natural selection; Environmental change; Isolation

14. (a) The fossil record has gaps and lets us see what organisms were like at an earlier time.
    (b) **Any two from:** Fossils are formed randomly; Not every step in an organism's development is recorded in the fossil record; The bacteria were still alive but fossils are not.
    (c) A mutation must have occurred.
    (d) **This is a model answer which would score full marks:**
    Selective breeding is where a breeder selects breeding pairs based on the desired characteristics that an organism has. The genes are already present – they just need to be selected. If the genes were already there, however, then the new characteristic would turn up regularly whenever the conditions for expressing that characteristic were right. However, in Lenski's experiment, it only appeared in one flask. Furthermore, the gene for the new characteristic would have been detected in the original cultures if it were always there, so the gene must have arisen because of a new, random mutation. This means that evolution has taken place in the flask and not selective breeding.
    (e) Go back to an earlier generation and see if the same mutation occurs again **and** Use technology to see how the DNA has changed **should be ticked**.

Module B4: The Processes of Life
(Pages 34–44)

1. B

2. protein **should be ringed**.

3. (a) The enzyme does not work / is denatured / is destroyed (at high temperatures) **[1]**. The active site / shape of the enzyme is changed; The active site / shape of the enzyme no longer fits the starch molecule (so the starch is not broken down / stays intact) **[1]**. **[No marks for 'The enzyme is killed'.]**
    (b) To make sure her results were repeatable, so that any difference was caused by the change in temperature. **[No marks for references to a 'fair test'.]**
    (c) **This is a model answer which would score full marks:**
    Chloe would need to use a minimum of five different samples of protein. She would then add a set amount of pepsin to the protein. She would need to keep the temperature and pH the same for each treatment. After a set time she would determine how much of the protein had been broken down. By repeating the experiment at a range of temperatures, she would be able to work out the optimum temperature for pepsin. The experiment would not work with starch because pepsin is an enzyme that is specific for protein. Starch is a carbohydrate and so would not be affected at all by pepsin.

4. **This is a model answer which would score full marks:**
    The cytoplasm is where anaerobic respiration occurs and where the enzymes needed for it are made. Aerobic respiration occurs in the mitochondria and the enzymes needed for it are made in these. The energy released by both anaerobic and aerobic respiration may be used for synthesising large molecules, such as polymers like proteins. It may be used as the activation energy for other cell processes, such as active transport.

5. (a) Carbon dioxide; Oxygen

(b) Chlorophyll
   (c) **Any one from:** It will not grow as much; It will go yellow; It will grow tall and skinny.

6. (a) 18
   (b) **Any two from:** The number of buttercups increases the further away from the trees; The number of buttercups increases steadily to 4–6 metres; The number of buttercups levels off beyond the 6-metre mark.
   (c) To increase the repeatability / reliability of the data / results.

7. **This is a model answer which would score full marks:** Seedlings A and C grew a lot in the warm places. Seedling D had grown a little and the shaded windowsill would not have been as warm as seedling A's windowsill. Seedling B had not grown at all in the cold. From these observations, Petra would have been right. However, seedlings C and D were both healthy-looking and had been exposed to light. Seedling A was looking very thin and yellow. Seedling B had not changed at all, so being in the dark had not caused it to grow. From these observations, Petra was wrong. Overall, based on her evidence, Petra could not make a firm conclusion as to whether it was light or temperature that had caused the differences. She would have to do more and improved experiments in order to establish this.

8. (a) Glucose + Oxygen ⟶ Carbon dioxide + Water (+ Energy) **[1 for correct reactants; 1 for correct products]**
   (b) **Any two from:** Anaerobic respiration does not need oxygen; Anaerobic respiration produces lactic acid; Anaerobic respiration produces less energy (per glucose molecule). **Or any two from:** Aerobic respiration needs oxygen; Aerobic respiration does not produce lactic acid; Aerobic respiration produces more energy (per glucose molecule)
   (c) (i) Enzyme
       (ii) **Any one from:** Protein; Amino acids

9. (a) (i) B
       (ii) A
       (iii) E
   (b) **Any two from:** Bacterial cells do not have a nucleus, whereas animal cells do have a nucleus; Bacterial cells have no mitochondria, whereas animal cells do have mitochondria; Bacterial cells have a protein / non-cellulose cell wall, unlike animal cells; Bacterial cells have plasmids / a circle of DNA, unlike animal cells.

10. (a) Fresh pineapple juice has something in it that makes the jelly disappear.
    (b) Tube A acts as a control / acts as a comparison / shows that other liquids / water do not affect the jelly.
    (c) (i) **Any one from:** Enzymes; Proteases
        (ii) **Any one from:** Destroyed it; Denatured it; Changed it; Stopped it working
        [No marks for 'Killed it'.]
    (d) The jelly would have disappeared more quickly in tube B **[1]** because there would be a greater surface area of jelly touching the pineapple juice **[1]**.

11. (a) Because it comes from living organisms
    (b) Because the bacteria respire anaerobically
    (c) Methane
    (d) **Any two from:** There is no need to dispose of the waste products it is made from in landfill sites; It does not add to acid rain / sulfur dioxide; It is carbon neutral / the carbon dioxide produced is balanced by crops planted to produce more biofuel; It reduces use of fossil fuels; It reduces the need to transport fuels around the world; It reduces pollution from oil spills, etc.; It is a renewable fuel.

12. (a) Carbon dioxide
    (b) Because the yeast will respire aerobically / with oxygen **[1]** and ethanol / alcohol production needs anaerobic conditions / no oxygen **[1]**.
    (c) It is needed for (both aerobic and anaerobic) respiration to take place.

13. Emily; Darren

14. (a) So that there would be no photosynthesis occurring **[1]** and any food reserves / starch in the leaf would be used up **[1]**.
    (b) In the inner / green part **[1]** because there is / are no chlorophyll / chloroplasts in the white part / no photosynthesis takes place / no light is absorbed in the white part **[or reverse if referring to the green part] [1]**.

15. **This is a model answer which would score full marks:** As well as the correct temperature, plants need carbon dioxide and light for photosynthesis. If there is a lack of carbon dioxide in the greenhouse, then carbon dioxide becomes a limiting factor. Burning wood makes more carbon dioxide available for photosynthesis. For example, the greenhouse may have 1 arbitrary unit of carbon dioxide, whilst burning wood may bring the level up to 4 arbitrary units, which means the plants have enough carbon dioxide for growth. However, smoke from the burning wood may end up blocking the light in the greenhouse, so then light becomes a limiting factor.

16. $6CO_2$; $6O_2$ **[1 for correct symbols; 1 for correctly balancing]**

17. (a) **Any one from:** Yes because the reaction happens most quickly at pH 1; No because there is no result for pH 2 or pH 3, so it is not possible to tell if the reaction would happen more quickly at these pH values.
    (b) **This is a model answer which would score full marks:** Enzymes have a specific shape that enables a specific substrate to fit into it, which then allows the reaction to take place. This is called the lock-and-key hypothesis. The enzyme is the lock and the substrate is the key. Denaturing is where an enzyme undergoes a permanent change in shape. It can be caused by high temperature or the incorrect pH. Once the enzyme has denatured, the substrate no longer fits into the lock and so the reaction cannot take place. In humans the stomach is at pH 1, so pepsin works best at this pH. If it did not, it would be inefficient.

18. (a) Osmosis
    (b) Active transport
    (c) Mitochondria are sites of aerobic respiration / provide energy for the process.

19. The movement of water from a dilute solution to a more concentrated solution **should be ticked**.

20. (a) $C_6H_{12}O_6 + 6O_2 \longrightarrow 6CO_2 + 6H_2O$ (+ Energy) **[1 for correct reactants; 1 for correct products; 1 for correctly balancing]**
    (b) Root cells can respire anaerobically / without oxygen.

21. (a) The potato took in water **[1]** because the solution inside its cells was more concentrated than the solution outside **[1]**.
    (b) The potato lost water **[1]** because the solution outside its cells was more concentrated than the solution inside **[1]**.

Module B5: Growth and Development (Pages 45–55)

1. **Lines should be drawn from** Egg **to** A female gamete; **from** Fertilisation **to** The fusion of a male gamete with a female gamete; **from** Sperm **to** A male gamete.

2. (a) Mitosis
   (b) So that the zygote / fertilised egg will end up with a whole set of chromosomes.

3. (a) Embryonic stem cells can be used to form any cell type **[1]**, whereas adult stem cells will only produce cells of a certain type **[1]**.
   (b) 8 cell stage **should be ringed**.
   (c) They start to become specialised.

4. Salivary amylase production **and** Membrane protein formation **should be ticked**.

5. (a) To replace damaged tissues
    (b) Adult stem cells

6. (a) mitosis **should be ringed**.
    (b) **Any suitable answers, e.g.** Plants continue to grow in height and width throughout their lives, whereas animals only grow in the early stages of their lives; Plants only grow at root / shoot tips, whereas animals grow in all areas of the body.

7. (a) **Any one from:** By being able to grow towards the source of light, the plants would be able to ensure the maximum light levels **[1]**, and grow well **[1]**; If the shoots grew away from the light rather than towards it, they would not get enough light **[1]**, and would die **[1]**.
    (b) Shoot D
    (c) Direction of sunlight

8. (a) **Any one from:** A; D
    (b) 23 **should be ringed**.

9. The parent cell divides by meiosis to form gametes **[1]**. Gametes from the male and female fuse during fertilisation **[1]**. Cells in the zygote divide by mitosis **[1]**.

10. double; base; gene; protein

11. (a) To ensure she could obtain repeatable results **[1]** and be certain that any difference was due to temperature only **[1]**. **[No marks for references to a 'fair test'.]**
    (b) The results up to 40°C did show an increase in cloudiness as the temperature increased.
    (c) No. The broth still went slightly cloudy at 50°C, so there was still evidence of growth at that temperature.
    (d) Yes. He could measure a difference numerically, rather than just through an observation.

12. (a) Mitosis
    (b) Meristems
    (c) If a cell is unspecialised, it has not yet developed into a particular type of cell.
    (d) Because all the cells are unspecialised **[1]**, so they can develop into all the different types of plant cell needed **[1]**.

13. Plant B has a longer stem to try to find light more quickly **[1]**. It has a bent stem in response to gravity / because the shoot grows upwards / against gravity **[1]**.

14. (a) Zygote
    (b) Meiosis
    (c) Mitosis
    (d) (Embryonic) stem cells

15. (a) Mitosis
    (b) Meiosis
    (c) Because they are gametes / sex cells / need to have half the chromosome number of the parent cell.

16. Amanda; Miriam

17. (a) (i) A tissue is a group of similar cells that carry out a particular function.
        (ii) **Any suitable example, e.g.** Cornea; Leaf epidermis; Palisade layer; Heart muscle
    (b) (i) An organ is a group of tissues that carry out a particular function.
        (ii) **Any suitable example, e.g.** Heart; Lungs; Leaf; Tree trunk; Stomach

18. **This is a model answer which would score full marks:** Embryonic stem cells can become any type of cell. Treating a patient with Parkinson's disease using embryonic stem cells means that the cells damaged by Parkinson's disease can be replaced with functioning ones. The treatment is used to minimise the suffering of a human being. Embryonic stem cells are harvested from embryos. Some people view these embryos as being people. They would argue that it is wrong to stop an embryo from growing in order to save the life of another. Scientists are developing techniques that enable adult cells to have the same ability as embryonic stem cells. This would mean the issue of using embryonic stem cells is removed.

19. (a) DNA has four bases: A, C, G and T **[1]**. These bases always pair A with T and C with G **[1]**. The order of these bases in the DNA strand is the genetic code for building up proteins from amino acids **[1]**.
    (b) A stomach cell will make pepsin because the base sequence **[1]** for this protein is switched on **[1]**. A skin cell has this sequence switched off, so it will not make pepsin **[1]**.

20. (a) (i) **The drawing needs to show a straight, taller shoot [1] with dots evenly spread on both sides of the shoot [1]**.
        (ii) **The drawing needs to show the shoot curving towards the light [1] with dots on the left-hand side of the shoot (i.e. the side furthest away from the light) [1]**.
    (b) **The drawing needs to show a straight, taller shoot [1] with an opaque cap over the shoot tip [1]**.
    (c) **Any two from:** The plant will grow towards the light **[1]** so it can photosynthesise more / make more food / glucose **[1]** for growth / fruit / seed development **[1]**.

21. The cell contains all the genetic material / code / DNA / genes **[1]**, so the genes for all the different types of cell are available in a body cell **[1]**.

22. (a) The order of the bases
    (b) Enzymes

23. (a) Root hormone
    (b) They affect cell division **[1]** at the tip of a shoot and/or root **[1]** and cause cells to grow in size **[1]**.
    (c) They are genetically identical.

Module B6: Brain and Mind
(Pages 56–67)

1. (a) Stimulus **should be ticked**.
    (b) (i) A reflex
        (ii) They are more likely to survive.
    (c) The Royal Mail delivery truck is red.
    (d) **This is a model answer which would score full marks:** Fiesa would introduce objects that are red, as well as other colours, to a number of territorial sticklebacks in fish tanks. Each non-red object would have to be the same size and shape as the red object. Fiesa would then count how often the territorial stickleback attacked each object that was introduced in the fish tank. She would repeat the experiment with each stickleback. She would then see if the number of times the red object was attacked was significantly higher than the attacks on the non-red objects.

2. (a) Reflexes of newborn babies
    (b) **Any one from:** The lower the birth weight, the lower the chance of passing the test; The greater the birth weight, the greater the chance of passing the test.
    (c) Step: The baby will make stepping motions when the sole of its foot touches a hard surface.
        Grasp: The baby will grasp and hold tight a finger placed into its palm.
        Startle: The baby pulls arms and legs inward after loud noise.
    (d) $0.29 \times 340 = 98.6$
        98.6 is rounded up to 99.
        [1 mark for correct working; 2 marks for 99 with or without working; 1 mark only for 98.6]
    (e) **Any one from:** Pupil reflex; Knee jerk; Dropping a hot object
    (f) Electrical
    (g) Hormones are chemical, whereas nerve signals are electrical; Hormone messages are slow, whereas nerve signals are fast; Hormone messages are long-lasting, whereas nerve signals are short-lived.

3. (a) **Lines should be drawn from** Receptor **to** Sensory neuron **to** Relay neuron **to** Motor neuron **to** Effector. **[1 for two correct lines; 2 for all correct]**
    (b) A reflex arc
    (c) (i) 0.9–3.1s
        (ii) She added up nine of the numbers (ignoring test 8) **[1]** and divided the total by nine **[1]**.
    (d) As the test number increases, the time taken to catch the £10 note decreases.

4. (a)

A	C	B	D

    [Accept 'C' before 'A']
    (b) This is the same experiment that Pavlov undertook **and** Humans are also animals **should be ticked**. [Both needed for 1 mark.]

5. (a) The nerve signals cannot travel past the break in the cord.
    (b) The sample size for this experiment is one **and** The mechanism behind the experiment is not understood **should be ticked**. [Both needed for 1 mark.]

6. (a) **A scatter graph should be plotted as follows: Neuron Diameter should be on the x-axis and Speed of Nerve Impulse on the y-axis [1]; All points should be accurately plotted [1]; A line of best fit (not joined dot-to-dot) should be drawn on the graph [1]**.
    (b) The greater the diameter of the neuron, the faster the impulse.
    (c) A fatty sheath **should be ticked**.

7. (a) billions **should be ringed**.
    (b) It increases
    (c) (i) By having a new experience
        (ii) By the experience being repeated
        (iii) They are deleted
    (d) Every time an experience is repeated, the neuron pathways are strengthened **[1]**. These pathways are more likely to transmit impulses, so you will learn how to do a task **[1]**.

8. (a) Physiological techniques study the effects of damage to different parts of the brain **[1]** in order to understand which parts of the brain control different functions **[1]**.
    (b) Magnetic Resonance Imaging (MRI) scanning
    (c) (i) The activities use different parts of the brain **should be ticked**.
        (ii) It prevents the scientists from introducing bias. They may be looking for evidence that the patient has responded 'yes' or 'no' where none exists.

9. (a) Group 1 **[1]**. The numbers have a clear pattern with group 1 **[1]** and there is no distraction to the process of remembering **[1]**.
    (b) **Any one from:** Remembering numbers is easiest if there is a pattern and no distractions; Remembering is most difficult when there is no pattern and there are distractions.
    (c) **Any one from:** Participants should be the same age / in the same age group; Participants should be the same sex; The tests should be carried out at the same time of day for each group.
    (d) The success rate of the groups should improve **[1]**. Over time they would adapt to the noise **[1]**.
    (e) It would enable the parts of the brain involved in memorising numbers **[1]** and coping with loud music to be identified **[1]**.

10. Insulin needs to affect the whole body but a nervous impulse does not affect the whole body **[1]**. The response needs to be long-term but nervous responses are short-term **[1]**.

11. (a) **This is a model answer which would score full marks:**
    Taste buds are spread all over the tongue and are the receptors that detect stimuli. The stimuli for the taste buds are the chemical taste particles that land on the taste bud when food substances are placed in the mouth. Each taste bud contains specialised cells with microvilli, which respond to the five different tastes. Sensory neurons send an electrical nerve impulse to the brain, where it is processed and interpreted. The person then perceives the taste as being either one taste or a combination of the five tastes – sweet, salty, bitter, sour and umami.
    (b) The tongue map idea was powerful and difficult to counter **and** The modern research took place a long time after the original research **should be ticked**.
    (c) Actual quantities could not be measured **[1]**. This meant that there was only a relative (proportional) indication of taste detection **[1]**.

12. (a)

C	E	A	D	B

    [2 for all correct; 1 for three letters in the correct sequence]
    (b) (i) Ecstasy / MDMA [accept 'Prozac']
        (ii) The sites where serotonin is reabsorbed into the sensory neuron are blocked.
        (iii) The nerve impulses would travel faster because the serotonin remains in the synapse.
    (c) Michael

13. (a) The benefit to the patient outweighs the risk of the operation **should be ticked**.
    (b) Her brain used different neuron pathways to carry out tasks.

Module B7: Further Biology (Peak Performance) (Pages 68–82)

1. (a) Support; Movement; Protection
    (b) **Lines should be drawn from** Ligament **to** Connects bone to bone; **from** Muscle **to** Contracts and relaxes; **from** Tendon **to** Connects muscle to muscle or muscle to bone; **from** Bone **to** Rigid tissue.
    [1 for each correct line up to a maximum of 3.]

2. (a) **Any one from:** Fever; Inflammation; The knee will be difficult to move.
    (b) It reduces friction between the bones.
    (c) (i) **Any suitable answers, e.g.** Any current medication she is taking; Alcohol / Tobacco consumption; Family medical history; Symptoms; Level of physical activity
        (ii) The treatment needs to take account of the patient's history, so that it does not make the problem worse and works in the most effective way.

3. (a) So that when muscles contract the bones move
    (b) To allow bones to move apart (when the joint moves)
    (c) **Any one from:** To reduce friction; To lubricate

4. (a) Not doing physical activity appears to be a result of fatness rather than the cause **should be ticked**.
    (b) 0.53 × 202 = 107.06 **[1]**
        0.25 × 107.06 = 26.77 **[1]**
        = 27 boys **[1]**
    (c) Increase the sample size; Look at the children over a longer period instead of just 7 to 10 years; Increase the time over which the children wear the accelerometer.
    (d) **This is a model answer which would score full marks:**
    You could argue that PE should be removed from the curriculum because, rather than lack of exercise causing a person to be fat (as would be the common sense view), the evidence suggests the reverse – being fat is the cause of lower physical activity. Therefore, having compulsory PE lessons is not the solution to the increase in obesity as it will not necessarily reduce someone's weight and the curriculum time could be used more productively. However, the sample size was low and the experiment only looked at a small period of time when the students were wearing the accelerometers. On the other hand, you could argue that PE should not be removed from the curriculum. Although the evidence seems to

suggest that the lack of physical activity is not a cause of being fat, there are still issues with the experiment. The sample size was low and the timescale when wearing the accelerometers was short. PE also provides advantages other than losing weight, for example, being part of a team involves communication, teamwork and learning new skills.

5. (a) $22.9 = $ Mass $\div (1.76)^2$
So mass $= 22.9 \times (1.76)^2 = 70.9$kg
[1 for correct working but wrong answer]
(b) As a measure of whether or not you are a healthy weight for your height.
(c) Exercise; Eat a healthier diet.
(d) 98kg – 77kg = 21kg **[1]**
21kg ÷ 2 months = 10.5kg per month **[1]**

6. (a) **Any suitable answer, e.g.** Dislocation; Torn ligaments / tendons
(b) **Any two from:** Swelling; Pain; Inability to move the joint
(c) **Any suitable answer which includes the following:** Resting the ankle so that pressure isn't put on it; Using ice to reduce inflammation; Compressing and elevating the ankle to allow excess fluid to flow away, reducing swelling.

7. (a) Ectoplasm **should be ticked**.
(b) Platelets
(c) Plasma **[accept 'red blood cells']**

8. (a) A: Right atrium; B: Right ventricle; C: Left atrium; D: Left ventricle
[1 for two correct; 2 for all correct]
(b) The left-hand side pumps blood to the whole body, whereas the right-hand side just pumps blood to the lungs **[1]**. More force is needed to pump the blood to the whole body rather than to just the lungs **[1]**.
(c) The blood would flow backwards in the heart **[1]**. This could cause an irregular heart beat and could lead to a heart attack **[1]**.
(d) **This is a model answer which would score full marks:**
The blood enters the right-hand side of the heart via the vena cava, filling the right atrium. It then passes through a valve into the right ventricle. It is then pumped through another valve to the lungs via the pulmonary artery. Once the blood has picked up oxygen, it returns into the left-hand side of the heart from the pulmonary vein into the left atrium. It then moves through a valve into the left ventricle. It finally leaves via the aorta to the rest of the body.

9. (a) **Any suitable diagrams, e.g.**

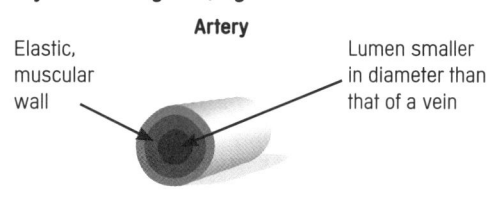

Artery
Elastic, muscular wall
Lumen smaller in diameter than that of a vein

Vein
Thin wall
Wide lumen

[1 for each appropriate diagram; 1 for appropriate labelling on each diagram]
(b) Capillary
(c) Artery
(d) Vein

10. (a) The more cigarettes smoked, the higher the risk of dying from heart disease; The older the person, the higher the risk of dying from heart disease.
(b) **Any three from:** Arteries get narrower / clogged / blocked; Less oxygen gets to the muscle; Less glucose / nutrients gets to the muscle; Less waste / carbon dioxide gets removed; Less respiration / energy released in the heart muscle.
(c) **Any one from:** Because if the usage is high, there is a higher risk of heart disease, so the programme needs to take this into account; If the usage is high, the amount of exercise should be less than if there is low or no usage of tobacco.

11. (a) brain; shiver; glands
(b) brain **should be ringed**.
(c) Energy gain and loss are almost balanced all the time **and** Respiration provides heat energy to balance any loss of heat from the body **should be ticked**.
(d) You will not be able to sweat as much **[1]**, so you will not be able to lose heat very well **[1]**.
(e)

| A | D | B | C | E |

[1 for each correctly placed up to a maximum of 3.]

12. (a) (i) Sweating / Perspiration **[accept 'vasodilation']**
(ii) The sweat draws heat from the body, cooling it down.
(b) Less than the temperature in his fingers **should be ticked**.
(c) **This is a model answer which would score full marks:**
Both Sir Charles and the egg are made of proteins. Sir Charles, however, survived because of homeostasis. He was able to actively adjust his body to account for the changes in temperature by getting rid of the excess heat. The egg, however, although made of protein, could not adjust its temperature and therefore cooked.
(d) Each person increased the sample size **should be ticked**.

13. (a) **Any one from:** Obesity; Poor diet
(b) Insulin unlocks cells; this allows glucose to enter **should be ticked**.
(c) By having a healthy diet
(d) The research is critically evaluated by other scientists who are experts in the field.
(e) Sugar in the urine
(f) **This is a model answer which would score full marks:**
As the person takes in food, it is digested and broken down into smaller molecules such as glucose and fructose. Insulin is released by the pancreas which 'unlocks' the cells, allowing the glucose to enter. When the glucose concentration drops, the level of insulin decreases. The graphs show that the insulin peaks after the sugar in the glucose peaks. This is because the insulin is released in response to the glucose level in the blood.

14. **This is a model answer which would score full marks:**
The blood from the artery carries dissolved oxygen at high pressure. The blood vessels get narrower and this slows down the flow of blood. Fluid from the plasma leaves and becomes tissue fluid. This provides the cells with the dissolved food and oxygen they need.

15. (a) **This is a model answer which would score full marks:**
Over the course of a day, Gurjit's mass would change. This is because she will gain weight from food and drink. When she excretes waste through urine and faeces, her mass would decrease. It is not, therefore, a good idea to take many measurements over a day. The data would be more reliable if she recorded her mass once a week at the same time. This would remove the daily variations, making the data more reliable and making it easier to see real mass loss.
(b) The scales are reporting 0.01kg accuracy. As her body mass is 7000 times higher, 0.01kg is too small a variation to be useful.
(c) BMI $= $ Body mass $\div$ (Height in m)^2
$= 69.5 \div (1.7)^2$
$= 24$
[1 mark for correct formula; 1 mark for correct calculation using average mass on February 9; 3 marks for correct answer without working]

16. (a) (i) Brown bread **should be ringed**.
    (ii) Brown rice **should be ringed**.
    (iii) Fructose **should be ringed**.
    (b) Carrots have vitamins the body needs.
    (c) Fat reserves broken down / Muscles increase / BMI decreases **should be ticked**.

17. (a) Homeostasis
    (b) hypothalamus; hypothalamus; nerve; vasodilation
    [1 for three correct; 2 for all correct]
    (c) There are two effectors which have opposite effects **[1]**. This enables a more sensitive and controlled response **[1]**.

Module B7: Further Biology (Learning from Ecosystems) (Pages 83–90)

1. (a) The waste from a part of the ecosystem can be used by other organisms **should be ticked**.
   (b) Inputs; Outputs **[Both needed for 1 mark.]**
   (c) **This is a model answer which would score full marks:** On the one hand, the people living in the Amazon are poor and need to use the forest for housing and logging so that they have space in which to live and can gain income from the wood sold. The Amazon supplies a number of ecosystem services such as resources, clean air, water, soil, minerals, nutrients, etc. However, if the people in the forest continued with deforestation, then the ecosystem services would be disrupted and the rainforest would decrease in size. Fewer trees would mean the soil would be more likely to be lost and the forest may die.

2. Microorganisms contain different enzymes **[1]** to break down the proteins, carbohydrates and lipids in waste **[1]**. The substances they release can then be used by plants **[1]**.

3. (a) The chance of successful fertilisation is increased; The number of offspring that survive to adulthood is increased.
   (b) (i) Flower
       (ii) Pollen
       (iii) Wind pollen would be much lighter as it would need to be blown / travel in the air.

4. (a) millions **and** biomass **should be ringed**.
   (b) The Sun originally supplied the energy for the plants, and the animals that fed on them, millions of years ago.
   (c) Farrah

5. (a) To attract insects for pollination.
   (b) …would be less able to adapt to environmental change; … would be less juicy; **and** …would be more variable in quality **should be ticked**. **[All three needed for 1 mark.]**
   (c) Not all the pollen will reach a plant that needs fertilising **should be ticked**.
   (d) If the tomatoes were eaten, the seeds would pass through the body undigested. This would mean that they were undamaged and able to grow **[1]**. Once out of the body, they would be out of the laboratory **[1]**. In the environment they would be able to compete with unmodified varieties **[1]**.

6. (a) Niamh
   (b) Arwen
   (c) (i) Peer review
       (ii) The findings may still turn out to be wrong **should be ticked**.

7. (a) The concentration of chemical substances builds up in each trophic level of a food chain.
   (b) Percentage increase
   $$= \frac{\text{Amount in osprey} - \text{Amount in large fish}}{\text{Amount in large fish}} \times 100$$
   $$= \frac{25 - 2}{2} \times 100 = \frac{23}{2} \times 100 = 1150\%$$
   [1 for correct working but wrong answer]

(c) The DDT causes the egg shell to become thinner **[1]**. This makes the eggs more likely to break, killing the chicks **[1]**.

8. (a) **Any suitable answer, e.g.** A situation in which the nutrient content is enriched to the point where the productivity of an ecosystem is excessively increased.
   (b) **This is a model answer which would score full marks:** The extra nutrients from the run-off caused bacteria and algae to multiply uncontrollably. The rapid growth, due to the high reproduction rate of the organisms, led to the dissolved oxygen being used up as the algae died and decomposed. Fish and other large organisms need high levels of oxygen to respire and so the reduction in oxygen concentration caused them to die.
   (c) Desertification

9. (a) **This is a model answer which would score full marks:** Sunlight was captured by plants via photosynthesis and animals consumed the plants. The plants and animals died and sank to the bottom of the sea, where they were covered with mud and subjected to huge pressure for millions of years. This caused the remains to turn into oil. The immense length of time it takes to form means that the oil is non-renewable (it does not go back into the ecosystem), so is not part of a closed loop system.
   (b) Scientists will help reach a decision based on evidence **should be ticked**.

Module B7: Further Biology (New Technologies) (Pages 91–98)

1. (a) **This is a model answer which would score full marks:** When Daniel is carrying out his experiment, he is selecting the bacteria that are breaking down the most plastic. He is effectively choosing the bacteria with the genetic mutations that allow this to happen. This is selective breeding. With cows, the same process takes place. This time the breeder is choosing the genes that lead to increased milk production.
   (b) Selective breeding
   (c) (Industrial) fermenter

2. (a) The gene for beta carotene is not present in rice to start with **[1]**. The gene for beta carotene is only found in carrots **[1]**.
   (b)

   | C | D | A | B | E |

   [1 for each correctly placed up to a maximum of 3.]
   (c) **This is a model answer which would score full marks:** With golden rice, the golden colour will only appear if all three genes are present. If one of the genes was missing, then the pigment would not be there, so it would be an easy visual check to see the success. With bacteria, another technique is to link the desired gene to another gene, giving antibiotic resistance. Only the bacteria carrying the gene would survive the application of the antibiotic. Sometimes a gene for fluorescence is linked. This means that the successful organisms will fluoresce under diagnostic conditions, indicating the presence of the desired gene.

3. (a) 1 to 100nm
   (b) There is a risk of infection with injection; The drugs are delivered to the precise place they are needed / Injected drugs would travel all over the body — not necessarily where they are required.
   (c) Georgina

4. (a) adult; donor; rejection
   (b) (i) The nerves connecting the legs and the brain have been severed **[1]**, so signals cannot pass up and down the spine **[1]**.
       (ii) **Any one from:** The stem cells could grow and connect the severed nerves together; The stem cells could become new nerve cells.

    (c) Valves **should be ticked**.

5. **(a)** Rice variety T has the poorest tolerance / does not tolerate salt water **[1]**. Rice varieties P and NB are affected approximately the same by salt water **[1]**.
    (b) The data for variety P has large error bars **[1]**. It may be better or equal to the performance of variety NB **[1]**.
    (c) 2011: 2 700 000 hectares
        2012: 2 700 000 × 1.03 = 2 781 000
        2013: 2 781 000 × 1.03 = 2 864 430
        2014: 2 864 430 × 1.03 = 2 950 363
        2015: 2 950 363 × 1.03 = 3 038 874
        3 038 874 hectares
        [1 for correct working but wrong answer.]
    (d) A huge amount of land is spoiled by salt water **and** Selective breeding takes longer than genetic modification **should be ticked**. **[Both needed for 1 mark.]**

6. **(a)** Samuel
    (b) Sample 3 / Fred's DNA
    (c) By the size of the molecule **[1]** and the charge **[1]**
    (d) To enable the sizes of the DNA fragments to be compared and calculated.
    (e) **Accept any answer between** 10 000 **and** 13 000 base pairs.

7. **(a)** Both recessive alleles are needed for the disease to occur.
    (b) DNA; white; probe **and** allele **should be ringed**.

8. **(a)** Embryonic stem cell
    (b) Embryonic stem cells are controversial because if they weren't used they could have grown into a human being.
    (c) The adult cells divide to become only that type of cell **[1]**. They have to be induced so that they can become any type of cell **[1]**.
    (d) **This is a model answer which would score full marks:**
        iPS cells can potentially be used to treat incurable disorders. Often there is a lot of suffering for the patient with an incurable condition. Using iPS cells could help to provide a cure and provide hope where there was none before. However, the risk is that the patient may end up getting a cancer, which may ultimately kill them. People have to balance the risk with the benefit and decide if it is worth taking.
    (e) The patients may have a different perception / personal view of the risk involved.

Growth and Development B5

(a) Which type of cell division does diagram A represent? [1]

(b) Which type of cell division does diagram B represent? [1]

(c) Why is it important that the new cells produced in the process shown in diagram B are different from the parent cell? [1]

16. A group of students is discussing cell division.

Amanda: Before the cells can divide the chromosomes must be copied.

Oliver: Mitosis is the type of division that produces gametes.

Charlotte: Cells produced as a result of mitosis have half the number of chromosomes as the parent cell.

Kieran: Mitosis leads to the tripling of the chromosome number.

Miriam: Genetically identical cells are the result of division by mitosis.

Which **two** students are making correct statements? [2]

_____ and _____

B5 Growth and Development

17. **(a) (i)** What is a tissue? [1]

   (ii) Give one example of a tissue. [1]

   (b) (i) What is an organ? [1]

   (ii) Give one example of an organ. [1]

18. Parkinson's disease is a disease that is incurable and causes suffering. Treatments are being developed that use embryonic stem cells to repair the damage caused by the disease. Embryonic stem cells are controversial. Give the arguments for and against using embryonic stem cells for developing a treatment for a patient with Parkinson's disease and suggest alternatives that are being developed.

The quality of written communication will be assessed in your answer to this question. [6]

Growth and Development B5

19. Genes are part of a strand of DNA.

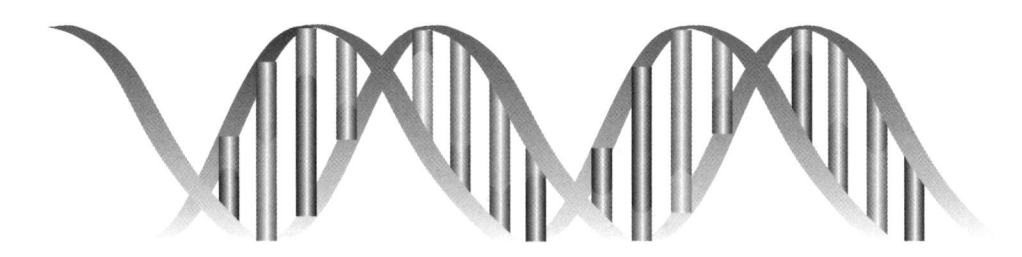

(a) Explain how a gene can cause a cell to make a protein. [3]

(b) Explain why a stomach cell will make the protein pepsin but a skin cell will not. [3]

[Total: .... / 66]

B5 Growth and Development

Higher Tier

20. (a) The diagram below shows a plant shoot. The dots show the location of auxin.

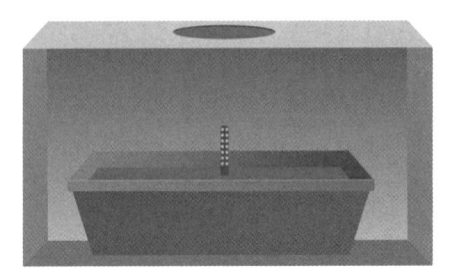

(i) On the diagram below, draw how the shoot will look after five days of light shining from the direction shown. Add dots to the shoot to show the location of auxin. [2]

(ii) On the diagram below, draw how the shoot will look after five days of light shining from the direction shown. Add dots to the shoot to show the location of auxin. [2]

(b) The diagram below on the left-hand side shows a plant shoot with an opaque cap placed over the shoot tip. On the diagram on the right-hand side, draw how the shoot will look after five days of light shining from the direction shown. [2]

Growth and Development B5

(c) Explain how phototropism increases a plant's chance of survival in natural conditions. [2]

21. In mammalian cloning, undertaken in a carefully controlled environment, a body cell can be induced to form a variety of different types of cell. Explain how this can happen. [2]

22. (a) DNA carries the genetic code. How is a single protein coded for in DNA? [1]

(b) The protein produced as a result of the DNA code is, most often, used by the cell to control a specific chemical reaction. What are the proteins that carry out this function called? [1]

23. (a) What should be applied to a cutting to encourage root formation? [1]

(b) How do auxins affect plant cells? [3]

(c) New plants grown from cuttings are **clones**. What does this mean? [1]

[Total: .... / 17]

B6 Brain and Mind

1. Sticklebacks are a type of fish. A male stickleback will attack any other male entering its territory. Biologists discovered that the male sticklebacks reacted to the red colour on the belly of the invading male. Sticklebacks demonstrate this behaviour even when kept in large fish tanks. Researchers noted that sometimes the sticklebacks got agitated when a red Royal Mail delivery truck drove past and was reflected in the tank!

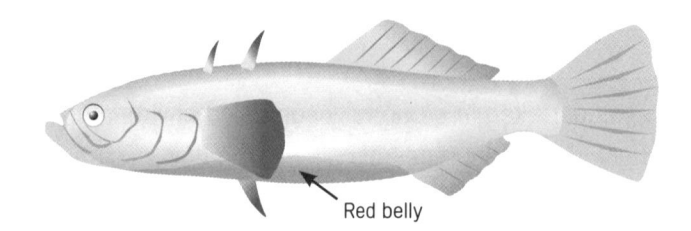

   Red belly

   (a) From the perspective of the home stickleback, the invading male with red on his belly is a change to its normal environment. What is the scientific term for this? Put a tick (✓) in the box next to the correct answer. [1]

   Variable ☐   Stimulus ☐

   Response ☐   Reflex ☐

   (b) The stickleback was responding rapidly and involuntarily to the invading stickleback.

       (i) What do we call this type of response? [1]

       (ii) Why do simple organisms respond in this way to changes in their environments? [1]

   (c) Why did the sticklebacks get agitated by the Royal Mail delivery truck driving past? [1]

   (d) Fiesa decides to try to prove it is the red colour that the stickleback is reacting to. Describe an experiment that she could carry out which would prove whether or not it is the red colour that the territorial stickleback reacts to.

       ✎ *The quality of written communication will be assessed in your answer to this question.* [6]

Brain and Mind — B6

2. A maternity unit at a hospital has provided data about newborn babies and their success in some tests.

Weight	Percentage of Newborn Babies Passing Test		
	Step	Grasp	Startle
Normal	98%	99%	100%
25% lower than normal	89%	92%	94%
50% lower than normal	70%	71%	69%

(a) What is the hospital testing for? [1]

(b) What is the correlation behind the results? [1]

(c) Briefly describe what each test involves. [3]

Step:

Grasp:

Startle:

(d) If the number of babies born with 50% lower-than-normal birth weight was 340, how many **failed** the grasp test? Show your working. [2]

(e) State one reflex that adult humans possess. [1]

(f) What type of signal is sent along neurons in the nervous system? [1]

(g) Give **three** differences between nerve signals and hormones. [3]

B6 Brain and Mind

3. Joss is cooking sweetcorn in the microwave. When he touches the cup, it is extremely hot and he drops the cup from his hand.

(a) The chart below shows a range of possible steps that took place which led to Joss carrying out this physical response. Draw straight lines between one box in each column to show the correct order of events. [2]

Message detected by...	Sent via...	Sent via...	Sent via...	Carried out by...
Receptor				Receptor
	Sensory neuron	Sensory neuron	Sensory neuron	
Effector				Effector
	Motor neuron	Motor neuron	Motor neuron	
Brain				Brain
	Relay neuron	Relay neuron	Relay neuron	
Relay				Relay

(b) What is this sequence called? [1]

(c) Claire decides to carry out an experiment to see how fast people's reactions are. She times how long it takes a person to catch a £10 note dropped between two fingers. The results are shown below.

Test	1	2	3	4	5	6	7	8	9	10
Time Taken (s)	2.0	2.1	1.9	1.7	1.6	1.6	1.5	3.1	1.2	0.9

(i) What is the **range** of values in Claire's experiment? [1]

(ii) Claire reports the mean as being 1.6s. Explain how she calculated this result. [2]

(d) Joss tells Claire that her data show a correlation. What is the correlation? [1]

Brain and Mind — B6

4. Pavlov was a scientist who discovered what is now called **conditioned reflexes**. His experiments on dogs showed how this type of reflex took place.

(a) The four stages, **A**, **B**, **C** and **D**, describe the processes involved in developing a conditioned reflex. They are not in the correct order. Put the stages in the correct order by writing the letters in the empty boxes. [1]

- **A** A bell is rung repeatedly whenever the dog is shown meat.
- **B** Eventually the bell is rung without meat present.
- **C** The dog is given the meat each time.
- **D** The dog salivates as if meat were present.

Start ☐ ☐ ☐ ☐

(b) In 2003, scientists showed that when humans were shown abstract images together with smelling either peanuts or vanilla essence, they then associated the images with peanuts or vanilla. This is a form of conditioned reflex. Why should this finding not be a surprise? Put ticks (✓) in the boxes next to the **two best** answers. [1]

This is the same experiment that Pavlov undertook. ☐   Humans are intelligent. ☐

Humans are also animals. ☐   Scientists published this before. ☐

5. Read the newspaper article below.

> **To Walk Again**
>
> In 2011, a man who had been paralysed from the waist in a terrible car accident was able to walk again. The man had severed his spinal cord in the accident. Researchers at an American university gave the man daily electrical impulses which, after a period of time, enabled him to move his legs again. The man is now learning how to walk again and has a new lease of life.

(a) Why are patients paralysed if the spinal cord is severed? [1]

....

(b) The researchers are claiming a breakthrough in reversing paralysis. However, other scientists urge caution, warning that it should not be assumed that everyone will benefit from this in the future. Which of the following are the two **best** reasons behind the warning? Put ticks (✓) in the boxes next to the best answers. [1]

Electricity is not available everywhere, so people won't necessarily benefit. ☐

The sample size for this experiment is one. ☐

The work needs to first win the Nobel Prize. ☐

The mechanism behind the experiment is not understood. ☐

B6 Brain and Mind

6. The table below shows the average speed that nerve impulses take travelling through neurons of different thicknesses.

Neuron Diameter (μm)	Speed of Nerve Impulse (m/s)
1	2
2	6
3	15
4	19
5	25
6	28

(a) Plot a **scatter graph** of the data on the grid below. [3]

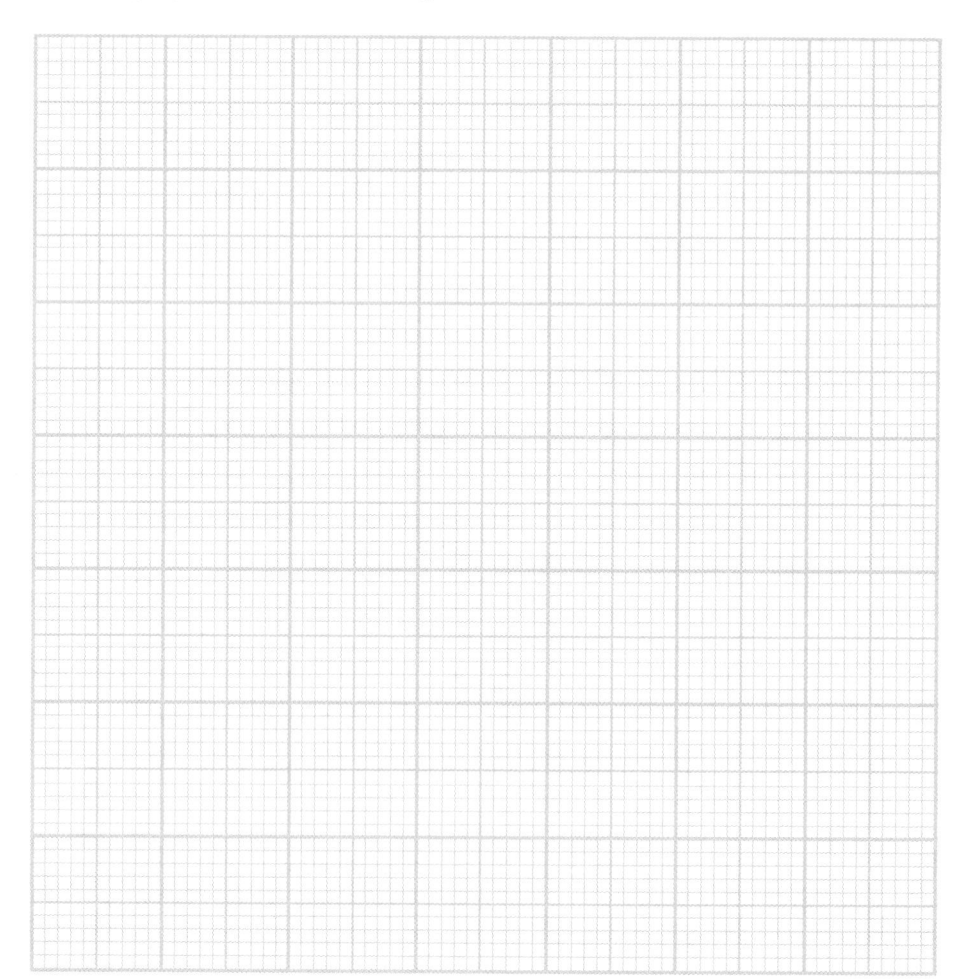

Brain and Mind — B6

(b) What conclusion can be made from the graph? [1]

....

(c) What gives the neuron an increased diameter? Put a tick (✓) in the box next to the best answer. [1]

A protein-based coating ☐   An insulation layer ☐

A plastic coating ☐   A fatty sheath ☐

7. (a) Mammals have complex brains. Approximately how many neurons are in a mammalian brain? Put a ring around the correct answer. [1]

      hundreds   **thousands**   **millions**   **billions**

(b) What happens to the number of synapses as the brain grows in the first years of life? [1]

....

(c) (i) How do the pathways between neurons become stimulated? [1]

....

(ii) How do the pathways become strengthened? [1]

....

(iii) What happens to the pathways that are not used regularly? [1]

....

(d) Explain why you are able to learn some skills through repetition. [2]

....

....

....

8. (a) Explain how physiological techniques are used to map the regions of the cerebral cortex. [2]

....

....

B6 Brain and Mind

(b) What technique was used to create this image? [1]

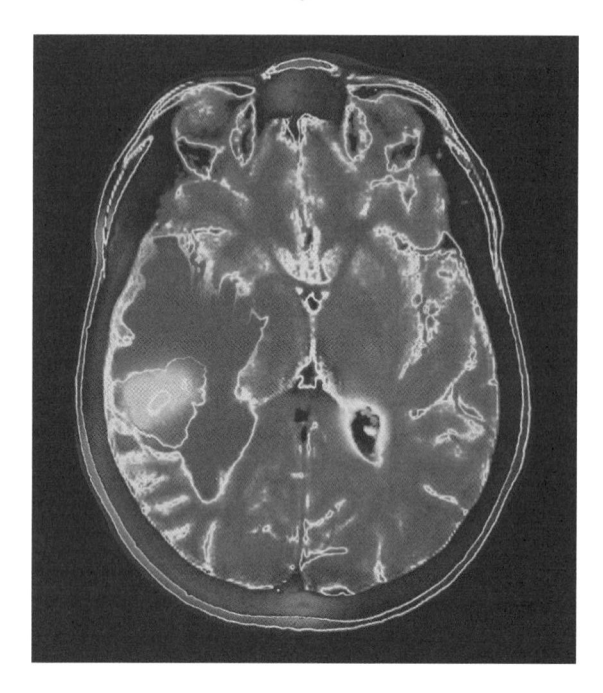

(c) Biologists at the Impaired Consciousness Research Group at the Wolfson Brain Imaging Centre are developing techniques to show whether people in comas retain any form of awareness. They do this by using an MRI scanner and asking the seemingly-unconscious patient questions about their life.

When carrying out the experiment the scientists ask questions, which only the patient and their family might know the answers to. The patient is asked to think about playing tennis for 'yes' and walking around the rooms of a house for 'no'. The doctors carrying out the study do not know the answers to the questions that the patient may or may not answer.

(i) Why did the scientists choose playing tennis and walking around the house as subjects for the patients to think about? Put a tick (✓) in the box next to the **best** answer. [1]

These were the scientists' favourite hobbies. ☐

The activities use different parts of the brain. ☐

The patients all play tennis. ☐

There is no difference between the activities in the brain. ☐

(ii) Why is it important that the scientists carrying out the experiment do not know the answers to the questions? [1]

Brain and Mind — B6

9. An experiment was set up to investigate how we remember information. Participants were given a set of numbers and asked to memorise them for 30 seconds. Some of the groups also had loud music playing as they memorised the numbers. The treatments for the experiment are shown below.

Group 1 (Quiet)	12342234	32344234	52346234	72348234
Group 2 (Loud Music)	12342234	32344234	52346234	72348234
Group 3 (Quiet)	12342297	22971234	22349723	39218475
Group 4 (Loud Music)	12342297	22971234	22349723	39218475

(a) Suggest which would be the most successful group in this experiment. Give **two** reasons for your answer. [3]

(b) Write a suitable hypothesis for this experiment. [1]

(c) Other than time to memorise, state a variable that it would be important to control for this experiment. [1]

(d) If the experiment was repeated for the same groups but with different numbers, what, if anything, would happen over time to the success rate of the groups which had loud music playing? Explain your answer. [2]

(e) The experiment is repeated by other researchers, this time using an MRI scanner. What added information would this procedure tell us? [2]

[Total: .... / 59]

B6 Brain and Mind

Higher Tier

10. Insulin is a hormone released from glands in the pancreas when its cells 'sense' blood glucose levels are high. Suggest why this response is more efficient than the brain transmitting nervous impulses to cause this to happen. [2]

11. The tongue is a sense organ that can detect a variety of tastes from the particles present in food. Taste buds contain specialised cells with microvilli, which respond to the different tastes.

In 1901, a German scientist, H.P. Hanig, tried measuring the relative sensitivity of the tongue to the then four basic tastes. Based on the statements of his volunteers, he came to the conclusion that the four tastes varied over the tongue, as in the diagram below.

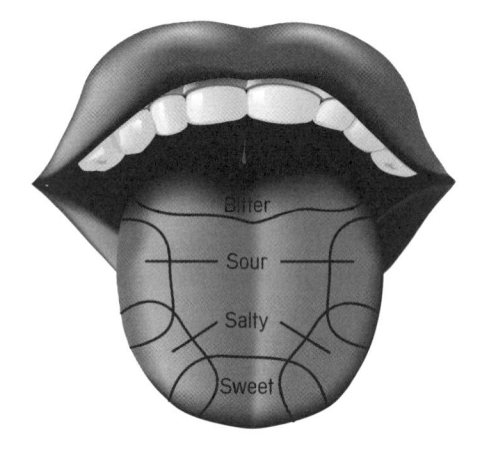

Hanig reported his findings in a graph but with no scale on the y-axis.

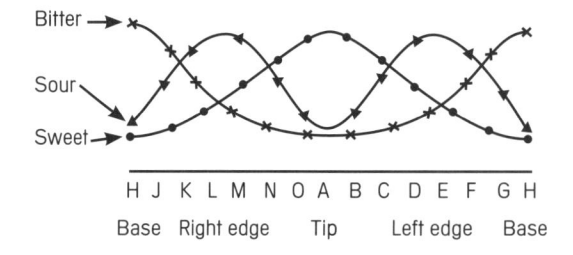

H J K L M N O A B C D E F G H
Base   Right edge   Tip   Left edge   Base

In 1974, Virginia Collings looked at the work again but concluded that the differences in taste receptors were negligible across the tongue. It is now accepted that each taste bud can detect a range of tastes (sweet, sour, salt, bitter and umami). There is no need to sub-divide the tongue into different areas.

Brain and Mind — B6

(a) Use the information provided and your own knowledge to explain how the taste bud detects taste and how the signal is transmitted to the brain.

The quality of written communication will be assessed in your answer to this question. [6]

....

....

....

....

....

....

....

....

....

....

(b) Although Collings disproved the original research in 1974, textbooks still continued to show the tongue-taste map into the 1980s. Which of the following explain why the fallacy of the tongue-taste map persisted for so long? Put ticks (✓) in the boxes next to the **two** best answers. [2]

The original research had been published. ☐

The tongue map idea was powerful and difficult to counter. ☐

The modern research took place a long time after the original research. ☐

People's tongues have changed over the years. ☐

(c) Suggest **two** ways why having no scale on the *y*-axis of Hanig's graph was such a problem. [2]

....

....

....

B6 Brain and Mind

12. A new drug, MIRI, has been produced that interferes with the neurotransmitter, serotonin. Biologists are trying to explain how the drug works by looking at how nerve impulses are affected in people taking the drug.

(a) The five stages, **A**, **B**, **C**, **D** and **E**, describe the normal process of nerve impulse transmission. They are not in the correct order. Put the stages in the correct order by writing the letters in the empty boxes. [2]

  A The serotonin fits into receptors on the relay neuron.

  B The serotonin is reabsorbed into the sensory neuron.

  C The serotonin is produced by the sensory neuron.

  D Once the receptors are all full, an impulse is initiated in the relay neuron.

  E The serotonin enters the synapse.

  Start | | | | | |

(b) Users of the new drug report that they feel elated (happy).

  (i) Which current drug is most like MIRI? [1]

  (ii) Suggest why the drug increases the concentration of serotonin in the synapse. [1]

  (iii) Why would this cause the effects noted? [1]

(c) The Government announces that it will ban MIRI. A group of friends is discussing the proposed ban.

Holly: I want to know the long-term medical effects of taking MIRI.

Lucy: I want to know how long MIRI stays in the body.

Michael: I want to know whether taking MIRI is good or bad.

Samuel: I want to know how much MIRI can be safely taken.

Who is asking a question that science **cannot** answer? [1]

_____

13. In 2007, it was reported that an 11-year-old girl, who suffered from an extremely rare and debilitating form of epilepsy, had undergone a hemispherectomy (an operation to remove half of her brain). The purpose was to remove the part of the brain that was causing the epilepsy.

Having had half of the brain removed, surgeons filled the cavity with sterile water so that the remaining half of the brain was supported. Surgeons do not fully understand how this operation works – it is amazing that the operation does not leave the patient senseless and immobile.

(a) What would be the basis for deciding whether or not to give a patient a hemispherectomy? Put a tick (✓) in the box next to the **best** answer. [1]

The prestige the surgeons get from carrying out the operation outweighs the risk of it. ☐

The benefit to the patient outweighs the cost of the operation. ☐

The benefit to the patient outweighs the risk of the operation. ☐

The benefit to the parents of the patient outweighs the risk of the operation. ☐

(b) The girl recovered the ability to speak and had no signs of the epilepsy following the operation. Suggest what happened in the brain to enable her to do this. [1]

_____

[Total: _____ / 20]

B7 Further Biology (Peak Performance)

1. **(a)** State **three** functions of the human skeleton. [3]

   1. _____

   2. _____

   3. _____

(b) Draw straight lines from the parts of the skeletal system to their correct functions. [3]

Part	Function
Ligament	Contracts and relaxes
Muscle	Rigid tissue
Tendon	Connects muscle to muscle or muscle to bone
Bone	Connects bone to bone

2. Margaret and Tiffany are in a doctor's surgery. Margaret has caught an infection, which has led to infected synovial fluid in her knees. She is in a lot of pain.

(a) Suggest what symptom, other than pain, Margaret will show as a result of the infection. [1]

_____

(b) What is the function of the synovial fluid? [1]

_____

Tiffany is recovering from back surgery. She is waiting for her first appointment with the physiotherapist.

(c) (i) Suggest **three** factors the physiotherapist would want to know about Tiffany before her treatment can start. [3]

   1. _____

   2. _____

   3. _____

(ii) Why would the physiotherapist need to know this information? [1]

_____

Further Biology (Peak Performance) B7

3. The diagram shows the muscles and bones of a human arm.

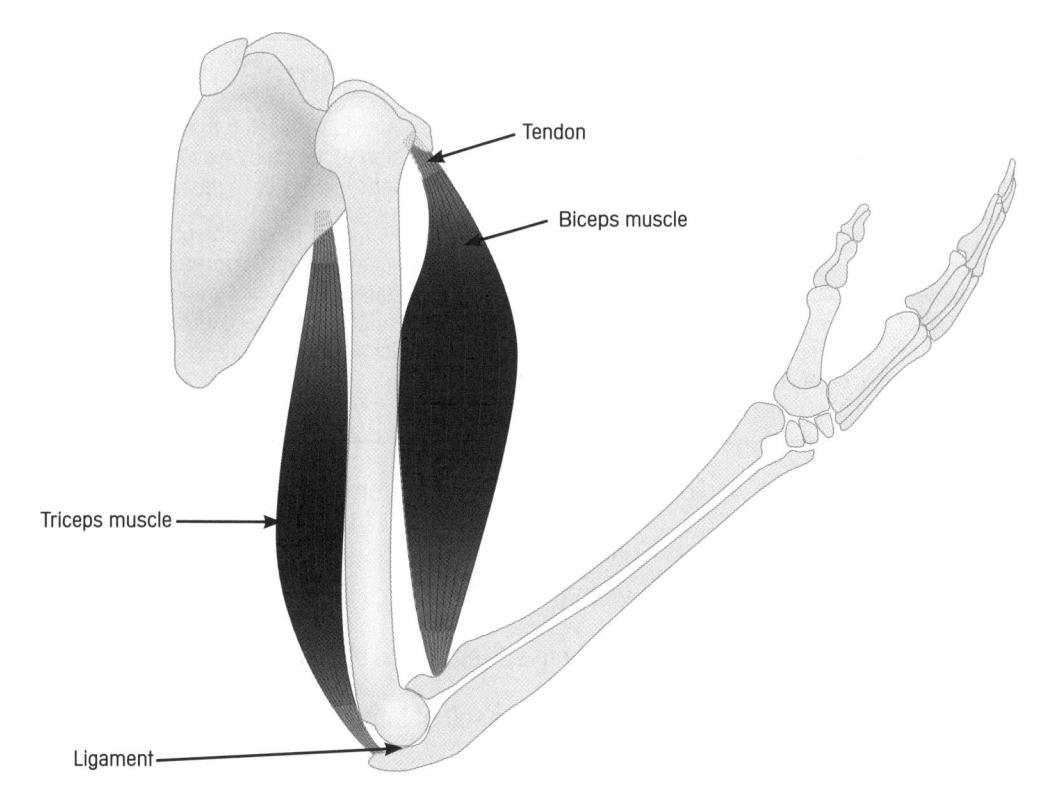

(a) Why is it important that tendons do not stretch? [1]

....

(b) Why is it important that ligaments are able to stretch? [1]

....

(c) At the elbow joint, the ends of the bones are covered with cartilage and the gap is filled with fluid. What function do the cartilage and the fluid have at the elbow? [1]

....

B7 Further Biology (Peak Performance)

4. Read the newspaper article.

> **Is PE a Waste of Time?**
>
> The increasing number of people who are obese is a time bomb. For many years it has been assumed that getting children to become more active would mean that obesity would drop. However, studies by a unit at the University of Plymouth have shown surprising results.
>
> The Early Bird study looked at children aged 7 each year until the age of 10. The children wore accelerometers, which recorded the amount of activity they undertook over a seven-day period each year. The children had their body fat measured by a specialised X-ray process.
>
> The findings indicated that the percentage of body fat at the start of the study was an indicator for predicting changes in physical activity over the study period.
>
> A 10% higher proportion of body fat at the age of 7 predicted a relative decrease in daily moderate and vigorous exercise of 4 minutes from the age of 7 to 10 years. More physical exercise at 7 years, however, did not predict a relative decrease in body fat over the same period.

(a) Which of the following would be the best conclusion from this experiment? Put a tick (✓) in the box next to the **best** answer. [1]

Physical activity makes you lose weight. ☐

Being fatter means you are more likely to suffer from diabetes. ☐

Not doing physical activity appears to be a result of fatness rather than the cause. ☐

Not doing physical activity makes you fat. ☐

(b) The study involved 202 children (53% boys) from 40 primary schools in Plymouth. 25% of the boys were classed as being overweight or obese.
How many overweight or obese boys were there? Show your working. [3]

(c) Give **three** ways in which this trial could be improved to make the results more reliable. [3]

1.
2.
3.

Further Biology (Peak Performance) B7

(d) Some people will say that compulsory PE in school should be removed from the curriculum as a result of this research, whilst others will say that it should not. Explain both sides of the argument, using evidence in the article to support the viewpoint.

The quality of written communication will be assessed in your answer to this question. [6]

....

....

....

....

....

....

....

....

5. Alex is 176cm tall and has a body mass index (BMI) of 22.9

(a) Use this equation to work out his body mass. Show your working. [2]

$$BMI = \frac{\text{Body mass in kg}}{(\text{Height in m})^2}$$

....

....

.... kg

(b) What is body mass index (BMI) used for? [1]

....

(c) If Curtis has a BMI of 27, what **two** things would you recommend he do to reduce it? [2]

1. ....

2. ....

B7 Further Biology (Peak Performance)

(d) Michael is overweight and starts a diet and exercise programme after Christmas. The graph below shows the weight loss over the period December to May.

Calculate the rate of weight loss from December to February. Show your working and give your answer in kg per month. [2]

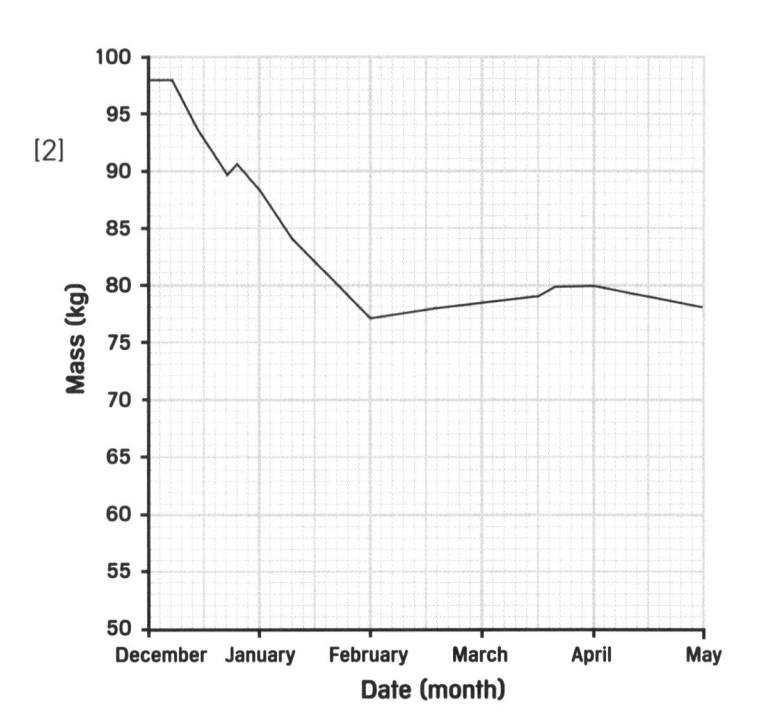

6. Sprains can be caused by excessive exercise.

(a) Other than sprains, what are **two** common injuries that can occur through playing sports? [2]

1.
2.

(b) Give **two** symptoms of a sprain. [2]

1.
2.

(c) Niamh has sprained her ankle. Her friend Emily says RICE is the answer. Explain what Emily means. [3]

Further Biology (Peak Performance) B7

7. (a) Which of the following is **not** a component of blood? Put a tick (✓) in the box next to the correct answer. [1]

Platelets ☐   Red blood cells ☐

Plasma ☐   White blood cells ☐

Ectoplasm ☐   Glucose ☐

(b) Which part of the blood bursts, releasing chemicals that trigger the conversion of fibrinogen to fibrin, forming a clot? [1]

....

(c) Which part of the blood transports substances around the body? [1]

....

8. (a) Label the following diagram of the heart. [2]

A ....   C ....

B ....   D ....

(b) Why is the left-hand side of the heart more muscular than the right-hand side? [2]

....

....

(c) Suggest what would happen if the valves in the heart were faulty. [2]

....

....

B7 Further Biology (Peak Performance)

(d) Starting with the blood entering the heart, via the vena cava, describe the route the blood travels as it goes through the heart.

✏ *The quality of written communication will be assessed in your answer to this question.* [6]

9. **(a)** In the space below, draw and label a cross-section of an artery and a vein. [4]

(b) Which type of blood vessel passes dissolved food and oxygen to cells in contact with it?
[1]

(c) Which type of blood vessel carries blood away from the heart? [1]

(d) Which type of blood vessel carries blood back to the heart? [1]

10. The chart shows a comparison between the number of cigarettes smoked and the percentage of deaths from heart disease in males.

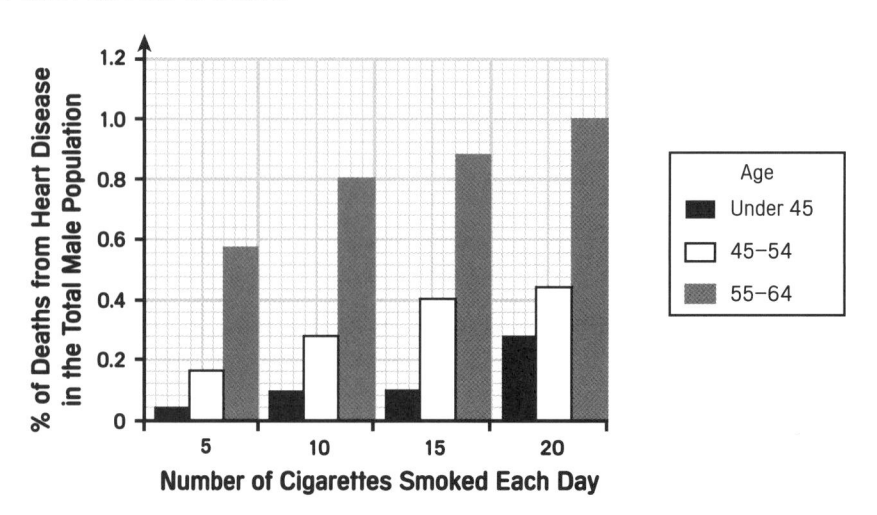

Further Biology (Peak Performance) — B7

(a) Using the information in the chart, suggest **two** conclusions about the factors that affect death from heart disease. [2]

1. ....

2. ....

(b) Smoking can cause fat deposits to build up in the coronary artery (the vessel supplying the heart muscle). Suggest **three** reasons why this might cause the heart to fail. [3]

1. ....

2. ....

3. ....

(c) A health professional is working out an exercise programme for a patient. Suggest one reason why the health professional needs to know the patient's cigarette/tobacco usage before working out the programme. [1]

....

11. This question is about temperature control in humans.

(a) Complete the following sentences about body temperature control. Use words from this list. [3]

shiver	stop	glands	muscles
pores	reduce	increase	brain

Temperature receptors in the skin detect the external temperature, while those in the

.... detect the blood temperature. If the body temperature falls too low, the

brain triggers muscles to .... and the sweat .... to

reduce the amount of sweat produced.

(b) Illness is often accompanied by a fever (high temperature). Fever is caused by the resetting of the temperature control centre. Where is this control centre found? Put a ring around the correct answer. [1]

skin   sweat gland   brain   pituitary gland

B7 Further Biology (Peak Performance)

(c) How do our bodies maintain a constant temperature of 37°C? Put ticks (✓) in the boxes next to the **two** correct statements. [2]

Energy gain and loss are almost balanced all the time. ☐

Body temperature is allowed to increase or decrease with the external temperature. ☐

When we are hot we sweat to keep the heat in. ☐

Respiration provides heat energy to balance any loss of heat from the body. ☐

Body temperature is maintained by moving to hot or cold places to balance heat loss or gain. ☐

(d) If you carry out very strenuous exercise, you may become dehydrated. How may this cause an extra increase in body temperature? [2]

(e) The following stages explain how the body controls its temperature. They are not in the correct order. Put the stages in the correct order by writing the letters in the empty boxes. One has been done for you. [3]

A Body temperature is too high or low.

B Instructions are sent from the brain.

C Blood flow to the skin increases or decreases.

D Receptors in the brain detect the rise or fall in temperature.

E Body temperature returns to the correct level.

A				

12. In 1775, Sir Charles Blagden heated up a room to between 115°C and 127°C. Sir Charles entered the room and survived in it for short periods of time. He later wrote in a scientific paper to the Royal Society: "The air felt very hot, but still by no means to such a degree as to give pain: on the contrary, I had no doubt of being able to support a much greater heat; and all of the gentlemen present, who went into the room, were of the same opinion."

(a) (i) What physiological process would have been taking place in Sir Charles's skin to enable him to survive in the room? [1]

(ii) Explain how this process works. [1]

Further Biology (Peak Performance) — B7

(b) When Sir Charles was in the room, what was his core body temperature? Put a tick (✓) in the box next to the correct answer. [1]

- The same as the temperature in his fingers. ☐
- Less than the temperature in his fingers. ☐
- Higher than the temperature in his fingers. ☐

(c) Why was Sir Charles able to survive in the room, yet a cracked egg cooked during the same period? Explain your answer.

✐ *The quality of written communication will be assessed in your answer to this question.* [6]

....

....

....

....

....

....

....

(d) Why did Sir Charles think it important to explain in his scientific paper that "all of the gentlemen present, who went into the room, were of the same opinion"? Put a tick (✓) in the box next to the correct answer. [1]

- Each person increased the sample size. ☐
- He wanted to show how popular he was. ☐
- This made the data more accurate. ☐
- Only males were involved in the experiment. ☐

13. Read the following article about diabetes.

Diabetes on the Increase

The incidence of type 1 diabetes in children is now double what it was in the 1980s and 10 to 20 times more common than it was 100 years ago, according to peer-reviewed research.

Levels of type 2 diabetes have been known to be rising for some time. This is the first time that type 1 (or juvenile) diabetes has been shown to be on the increase.

There are a number of hypotheses that have been put forward for this rise. Here are two of these:

- The sunshine hypothesis suggests that children today are in the sun less and so make less vitamin D. Vitamin D deficiency has been linked with type 1 diabetes.

- The cow's milk hypothesis suggests that exposure to cow's milk during the first six months of life affects the immune system and increases the risk of developing type 1 diabetes.

B7 Further Biology (Peak Performance)

(a) The article states that levels of type 2 diabetes have been rising for some time. What is the cause of type 2 diabetes? [1]

(b) Insulin has to be injected when a person suffers from type 1 diabetes. What does insulin do? Put a tick (✓) in the box next to the **best** answer. [1]

Insulin unlocks blood cells; this allows glucose to enter. ☐

Insulin is a hormone that makes you want to eat sugar. ☐

Insulin prevents glucose from entering cells. ☐

Insulin unlocks cells; this allows glucose to enter. ☐

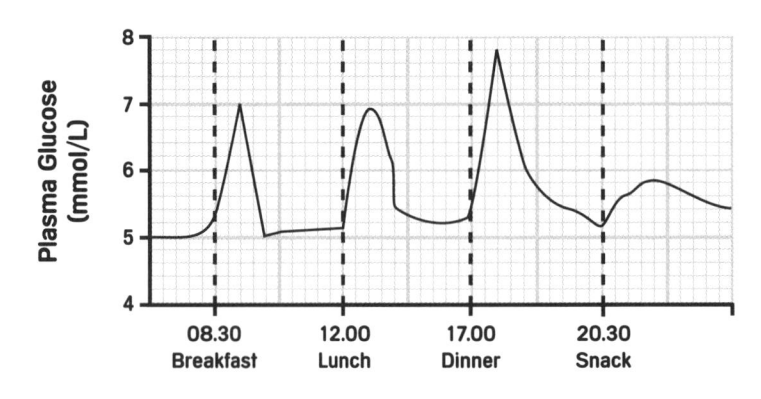

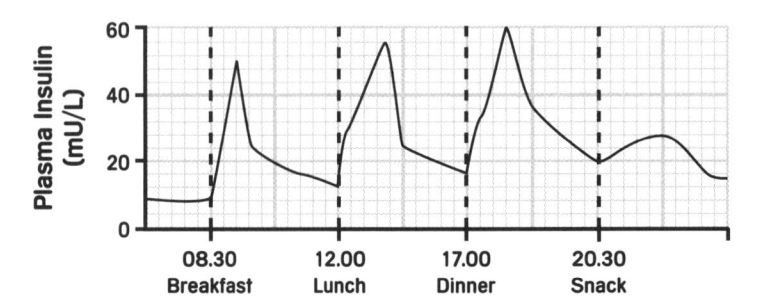

(c) How do you control type 2 diabetes? [1]

(d) The article states that the findings are from **peer-reviewed research**. What does this term mean? [1]

(e) The full name for diabetes is diabetes mellitus, which literally means 'sweet fountain'. What symptom does this refer to? [1]

(f) The graphs show blood sugar levels and insulin levels throughout the day.

Further Biology (Peak Performance) — B7

Why does the level of insulin in the blood change throughout the day? Use information from the graphs, along with the words **digested**, **glucose** and **pancreas**, in your answer.

✎ *The quality of written communication will be assessed in your answer to this question.* [6]

[Total: .... / 102]

Higher Tier

14. The diagram below shows a capillary bed.

Body cells

Capillaries

Describe and explain what happens when blood arrives at a capillary bed from an artery.

✎ *The quality of written communication will be assessed in your answer to this question.* [6]

B7 Further Biology (Peak Performance)

15. Gurjit decides to try to lose weight. She decides to monitor her body mass and takes a number of readings. A selection of readings is given in the table below.

Date	Time	Mass (kg)
February 9	7.01am	67.43
February 9	12.00pm	70.05
February 9	6.00pm	71.10
February 9	9.30pm	69.45
February 10	8.00am	68.44
February 10	11.30am	69.90
February 10	3.00pm	71.13
February 10	7.00pm	71.70
February 11	6.30am	70.00
February 11	1.00pm	69.19
February 11	6.15pm	70.12
February 11	10.00pm	71.10

(a) Gurjit was taking many readings of her mass over the week. There are many reasons why her mass would change through the day. Suggest why her mass would change and whether it is a good idea for her to take so many readings of her mass. Give a more reliable timescale for recording her mass. Explain your answer.

The quality of written communication will be assessed in your answer to this question. [6]

Further Biology (Peak Performance) B7

(b) Gurjit has recorded her mass to two decimal places. Explain why this is not necessary. [1]

(c) Gurjit is 170cm tall. What was her BMI for February 9? Show your working. [3]

16. Colin has type 2 diabetes, and he has decided to exercise regularly and change his diet. He is following a popular low GI diet. GI stands for glycemic index and is a measure of how easy it is to digest the carbohydrates in the food. The more complex the carbohydrate, the lower the GI. Carbohydrates that are easier to digest are more likely to cause weight gain than those that take a longer time.

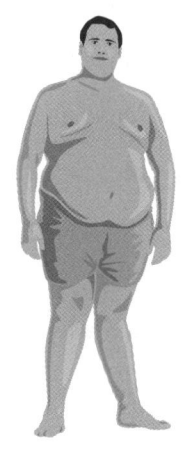

(a) The table below shows the GI values of various foods.

Food	GI	Food	GI
White bread	72	Carrots	92
Brown bread	69	Peas	40
Potato	80	Apple	39
White rice	72	Orange	40
Brown rice	66	Raisins	64
Pasta	50	Peanuts	10
Whole wheat pasta	41	Glucose	100
Cornflakes	80	Fructose	10

B7 Further Biology (Peak Performance)

Which type of food should Colin choose to eat from each of these pairs? Put a ring around the correct response.

(i) White bread / Brown bread [1]

(ii) White rice / Brown rice [1]

(iii) Glucose / Fructose [1]

(b) Carrots have a very high GI rating. Why is it wrong to say that Colin should not eat carrots as part of his diet? [1]

(c) As well as changing his diet, Colin is exercising regularly. What will happen to his body? Put a tick (✓) in the box next to the correct answer. [1]

Fat reserves broken down	Muscles decrease	BMI decreases	☐
Fat reserves broken down	Muscles increase	BMI decreases	☐
Fat reserves broken down	Muscles decrease	BMI increases	☐
Fat reserves built up	Muscles decrease	BMI decreases	☐
Fat reserves built up	Muscles increase	BMI increases	☐

17. Ollie is taking part in a marathon. It is a very hot day and Ollie has run 15 miles. His body is maintaining a constant core temperature.

(a) What is the technical term for the reason why Ollie's core body temperature is constant throughout the marathon? [1]

(b) Use words from the following list to complete the sentences. Each word may be used once, more than once, or not at all. [2]

**hormone   hypothalamus   nerve
vasoconstriction   vasodilation**

Ollie's blood temperature is detected by receptors in his _____.

The _____ sends a _____ signal to effectors in blood vessels, which carry out the process of _____.

(c) Explain what is meant by the term **antagonistic effectors** and why they are needed. [2]

[Total: ____ / 26]

Further Biology (Learning from Ecosystems) B7

1. **(a)** There is a saying 'One man's waste is another man's treasure'. In what way is this saying appropriate when looking at an ecosystem? Put a tick (✓) in the box next to the **best** statement. [1]

   Ecosystems have resources that make people rich. ☐

   Valuable drugs have been discovered in rainforests. ☐

   The waste from a part of the ecosystem can be used by other organisms. ☐

   Organisms are linked together in food chains. ☐

   (b) The Amazon rainforest in South America is an example of a stable ecosystem. What **two** things must be balanced in a stable ecosystem? [1]

   _____ and _____

   (c) Humans are having an impact on the Amazon rainforest. The main causes of deforestation are human settlements and logging. Between 2000 and 2006, the Brazilian part of the forest lost 150 000km², an area bigger than Greece.

   Explain the arguments for and against the creation of new homes and logging in the Amazon rainforest. Use the term **ecosystem services** in your answer.

   ✎ *The quality of written communication will be assessed in your answer to this question.* [6]

2. Explain how microorganisms break down waste and why this can help plants to grow. [3]

B7 Further Biology (Learning from Ecosystems)

3. The goal of living things is to survive and reproduce, producing offspring that survive until adulthood to repeat the process.

   (a) Suggest **two** reasons why males and females of different species usually produce sperm and eggs in large numbers. [2]

   1. ....

   2. ....

   (b) Flowers cannot move around to find a partner. Instead they have to use other strategies to successfully reproduce.

   (i) What organ is used to attract insects? [1]

   ....

   (ii) What reproductive structure is transported by wind or by insect from plant to plant? [1]

   ....

   (iii) For your answer to part **(ii)**, suggest a reason why there would be a difference between the mass of the reproductive structure of a wind and an insect-pollinated plant. [1]

   ....

4. **(a)** Put a ring around the correct options in these sentences about crude oil. [2]

   Crude oil is formed from the remains of plants and animals that died **hundreds / thousands / millions** of years ago. The **biome / biomass / bacteria** is covered by silt and rock and subjected to immense pressure and heat.

   (b) Explain the following statement:

   'When we burn oil, we are effectively burning fossil sunlight energy'. [1]

   ....

Further Biology (Learning from Ecosystems) B7

(c) A group of students is discussing the building of the Three Gorges Dam in China.

Amber
The dam should never have been built. Loss of animal and plant life is never acceptable.

Karim
The people will benefit as there was a shortage of water and energy.

Farrah
Decisions like this have to involve scientists to advise on the advantages and disadvantages.

Ges
Humans should always come first.

Who is making a statement which indicates that environmental issues should be consulted on? [1]

B7 Further Biology (Learning from Ecosystems)

5. Read the following article.

A Brief History of the Tomato

The tomatoes that we buy from supermarkets have an interesting story. For a start, they are not vegetables but fruit! Tomatoes are classed in the kitchen as being vegetables mainly because of the way we cook with them.

The original ancestor of the tomato needed to be cross-pollinated. The flower was a bright colour to enable this to take place. Modern varieties undergo a version of self-pollination. They need vibration to enable the pollen to transfer properly. This vibration can come from insects, such as bumblebees, or be applied by an 'electric bee'.

In 1994, a genetically-modified tomato, Flavr Savr, was released. It was claimed that this genetically-modified tomato had a longer shelf-life. This turned out to be incorrect and genetically-modified tomatoes can no longer be bought.

During the development process, the scientists were not allowed to eat the tomatoes.

When tomatoes are eaten, the seeds pass through the body undigested. This means that they land in ready-made manure.

(a) Why are tomato flowers a bright colour? [1]

_____

(b) What would be the disadvantages of tomatoes grown after cross-pollination compared with modern self-pollination? Put ticks (✓) in the boxes next to the correct answers. [1]

With cross-pollination the tomatoes…

   …would be less variable. ☐

   …would be less able to adapt to environmental change. ☐

   …would be less juicy. ☐

   …would be more variable in quality. ☐

(c) Why do flowers produce large quantities of pollen? Put a tick (✓) in the box next to the best answer. [1]

   There are a large number of flowers that need fertilising. ☐

   Pollen deteriorates quickly. ☐

   Not all the pollen will reach a plant that needs fertilising. ☐

   To cause hay fever in humans. ☐

Further Biology (Learning from Ecosystems) B7

(d) The scientists were not legally allowed to eat the genetically modified (GM) tomatoes. This was not because the tomatoes could have been poisonous or otherwise harmful to a human. Suggest why eating GM tomatoes could pose a threat to the environment. [3]

....

....

....

....

6. A group of students is talking about plants.

Ethan
Roots are there purely for the absorption of water.

Arwen
A study has been published which shows there is evidence that cutting down trees can lead to desertification.

Niamh
Roots have a dual function: they provide a way for water to get into the plant and they bind the soil together.

Claude
I can't see how cutting down trees has any effect on the landscape other than to make it less pretty.

B7 Further Biology (Learning from Ecosystems)

(a) Which student gives the best explanation of how roots work? [1]

(b) Which student refers to evidence for their argument? [1]

(c) (i) What process must a scientific paper go through before it is accepted for publication? [1]

(ii) Once a paper has been published, which statement is now definitely true? Put a tick (✓) in the box next to the correct statement. [1]

The findings are correct and will add to scientific knowledge. ☐

The findings may still turn out to be wrong. ☐

There is a 50% chance of the findings being wrong. ☐

The authors of the paper will earn royalties. ☐

[Total: .... / 30]

Higher Tier

7. DDT was the world's first synthetic pesticide.

DDT shows the ability to bioaccumulate. Eventually this caused the death of a wide range of organisms. One of the effects is that it makes egg shells thinner than they should be.

(a) What is meant by the term **bioaccumulation**? [1]

(b) The diagram shows a food chain.

Water → Zooplankton → Small fish → Large fish → Osprey

0.000 003ppm   0.04ppm   0.5ppm   2ppm   25ppm

DDT concentration (parts per million)

Further Biology (Learning from Ecosystems) B7

Calculate the percentage increase in DDT between the large fish and the osprey. Show your working. [2]

.... %

(c) Why would the accumulation of DDT cause the number of ospreys to decrease? [2]

8. In the 1960s and 70s, Lake Erie, one of the largest lakes in North America, was recognised as being a 'dead lake'. It had been swamped by the run-off from different farms and heavy industry surrounding the lake. Forty years after the run-off had been stopped, Lake Erie is on the way to recovery, although it has still not completely recovered.

(a) What is the definition of the term **eutrophication**? [1]

(b) Suggest why the fish in Lake Erie died. Explain your answer.

The quality of written communication will be assessed in your answer to this question. [6]

(c) What is the name of the process by which farming and overgrazing causes the soil to be washed away? [1]

B7 Further Biology (Learning from Ecosystems)

9. Using fossil fuels, such as oil, has an impact on the environment.

(a) Explain how oil is formed and why it is not part of a closed loop system.

The quality of written communication will be assessed in your answer to this question. [6]

(b) A new source of energy is discovered. It is located in an area of rainforest. Which statement represents the role of scientists? Put a tick (✓) in the box next to the **best** statement. [1]

Scientists know how best to use the new resource. ☐

Scientists are in it only for the money. ☐

Scientists always go against what the public believe. ☐

Scientists will help reach a decision based on evidence. ☐

[Total: .... / 20]

Further Biology (New Technologies) — B7

1. Each year 500 billion plastic bags are manufactured, the majority of which are wasted and end up in landfill sites. In 2009, a teenager in the United States, Daniel Burd, decided to try to grow a bacterium that could speed up the decomposition of plastic as a school project. He put ground plastic into boiling tubes filled with a yeast solution, which encouraged bacterial growth. Every day he sub-cultured from the tube where the greatest amount of plastic had been degraded. After several weeks, he had a bacterial solution which could degrade plastic by 43% in six weeks. Normally the same plastic takes over a thousand years to degrade.

(a) Explain how Daniel Burd's experiment is similar to breeding cows that produce more milk.

The quality of written communication will be assessed in your answer to this question. [6]

(b) Daniel Burd was carrying out a particular process to arrive at the final bacterial type. What is it called? [1]

(c) If Daniel Burd's bacteria were to be used on an industrial scale, what piece of equipment would be needed to culture large quantities of identical bacteria? [1]

2. Golden rice is a genetically modified (GM) variety of rice that contains extra genes enabling it to produce beta carotene. Beta carotene is found in carrots and gives them their orange colour. Inside the body, beta carotene is metabolised to produce vitamin A.

There are three extra genes added to the GM rice. Two are from daffodils and the other from a bacterium. All three are needed to make beta carotene.

(a) Why is it necessary to genetically engineer the rice rather than selectively breeding rice? [2]

B7 Further Biology (New Technologies)

(b) Genetic modification follows a sequence of steps. The statements below are about the first daffodil gene. They are not in the correct order. Put the steps in the correct order by writing the letters in the empty boxes. One has been done for you. [3]

A The plasmid is passed into a soil bacterium.

B Replication takes place.

C The gene is selected and isolated.

D The gene is inserted into a bacterial plasmid.

E The soil bacterium infects the rice plant.

C				

(c) Once a biologist has managed to insert the desired genes into golden rice, they then have to prove that the genes are there. Discuss the different ways that can be used to prove whether or not a gene has been incorporated into different organisms.

The quality of written communication will be assessed in your answer to this question. [6]

3. Atherosclerosis is a disease that can lead to heart failure. It results from eating a high-cholesterol diet. When an artery gets damaged due to the high pressure of the blood normally flowing through it, the cholesterol causes the normal healing process to form an atheroma. The atheroma narrows the artery, increasing blood pressure.

One way that biologists are looking to treat sufferers of atherosclerosis is to use nanotechnology. Liposomes can be created to deliver drugs directly to the site of the atheroma, so that it can be broken down before too much damage is done. Other nanoparticles containing iron can be used to visualise the atheroma in an MRI scanner.

(a) What is the size range that nanotechnology operates within? [1]

Further Biology (New Technologies) B7

(b) What two advantages do liposomes have over injecting the drugs directly into the body? [2]

1. ....

2. ....

(c) A group of students is discussing nanotechnology.

Harvey: Normal technology works well as it is. There is no need for new technologies.

Molly: We don't need other technologies. The ones we currently use are fine.

Georgina: If the majority of people will benefit from nanotechnology, then we should consider it, even if there are risks.

Louis: Everything could turn to grey goo! All research should be stopped just in case.

Which student is making an ethical argument? [1]

....

4. (a) Stem cells are being investigated to treat leukaemia, a disease that kills white blood cells. With the white blood cells dead, the body is open to infection as the immune system no longer works.

Complete the following sentences. Use words from this list. [3]

rejection   adult   embryonic   illness   donor   blood   recipient

Blood cells are made from the body's own .... stem cells in the bone

marrow. With traditional treatments, the marrow has to be removed and replaced with that from a

tissue matched .... The advantage of using stem cells from the patient's

own body is that the chance of .... is removed.

B7 Further Biology (New Technologies)

(b) Stem cells are also being used to try to cure spinal injuries.

   (i) Why can't people who are paralysed walk? [2]

   (ii) How could using stem cells help? [1]

(c) Technology has been developed to replace organs with mechanical versions. A pacemaker is designed to keep the heart beating.

   What other part of the heart can be replaced using biomedical engineering? Put a tick (✓) in the box next to the correct answer. [1]

   Coronary veins ☐   Valves ☐
   Heart strings ☐   Coronary arteries ☐

5. Rice is an important cereal crop in Pakistan, forming part of the local staple diet. Rice is also exported and earns the country some £26 million annually. However, rice cultivation is constrained by salinity. About 2.7 million hectares of cultivated agricultural land are affected by this problem, and the area affected is increasing at a rate of 3% per year. Biologists are trying to breed varieties of rice that can tolerate salt water.

   Three varieties of rice, **T**, **P** and **NB**, were tested. The graphs below show the response of the varieties to salt water.

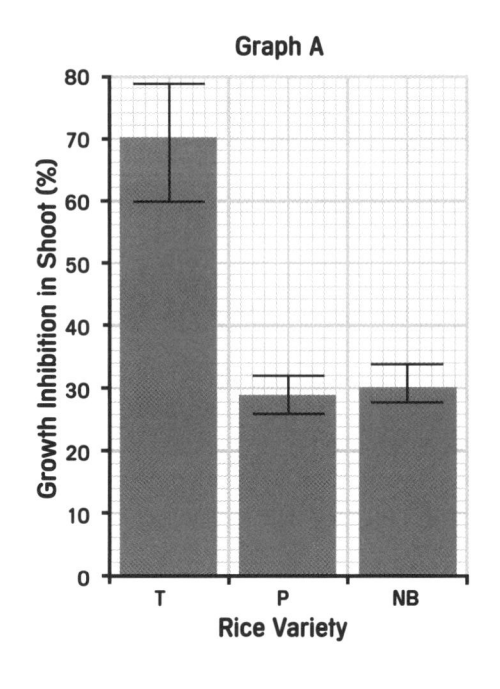

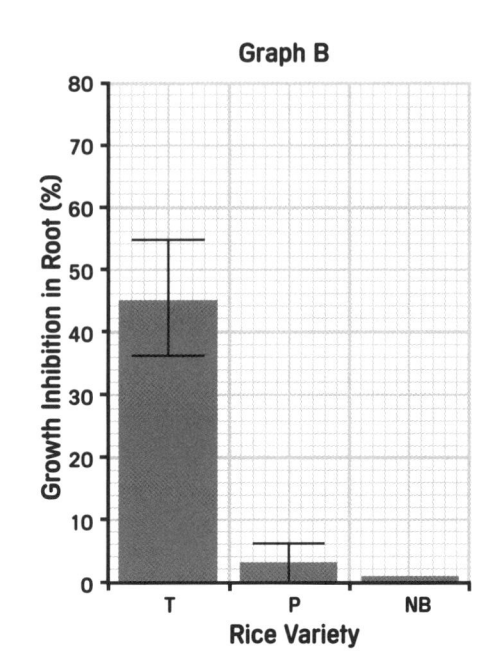

Further Biology (New Technologies) — B7

(a) What conclusion can be drawn from the results? [2]

(b) Tiffany says that variety NB has the least root-growth inhibition. Using the data in graph B, suggest why this is **not** necessarily true. [2]

(c) If the area of agricultural land affected by salinity was 2.7 million hectares in 2011, how many hectares would be affected in 2015? Show your working. [2]

(d) There is the possibility of genetically modifying rice with a gene from a salt-loving plant, so that rice can be grown in salt water. Why might scientists attempt to do this? Put ticks (✓) in the boxes next to the **two best** statements. [1]

Money is the priority for scientists. ☐

A huge amount of land is spoiled by salt water. ☐

Selective breeding takes longer than genetic modification. ☐

Scientists like to play God. ☐

[Total: .... / 37]

B7 Further Biology (New Technologies)

Higher Tier

6. At a crime scene, traces of DNA are detected. There are two main suspects, Samuel and Fred, both of whom claim they have never been at the site. Scientists carry out the process of southern blotting (separating DNA). The diagram shows a southern blot made by forensic scientists working on the case.

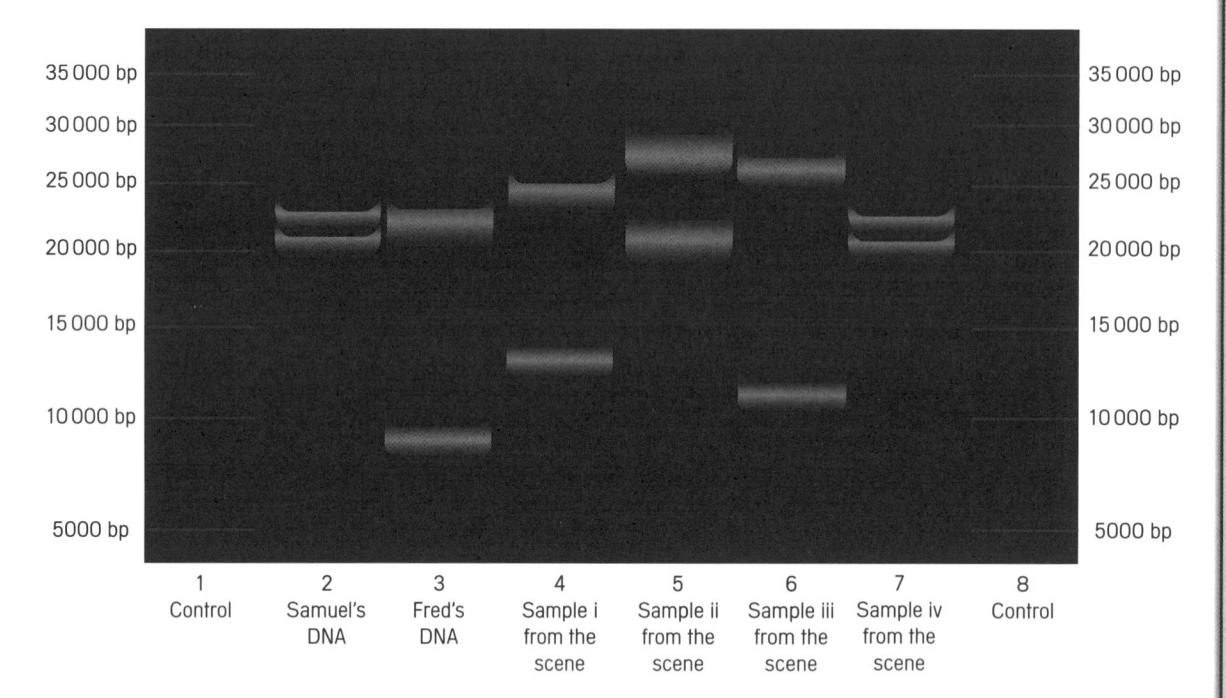

(a) Which suspect was at the crime scene? [1]

(b) Apart from the control, which sample contains the smallest DNA fragments? [1]

(c) In southern blotting how are DNA fragments separated? [2]

(d) What is the purpose of the control? [1]

(e) The control sample has seven DNA fragments. The fragment that travelled the furthest was 5000 base pairs long and the next furthest was 10 000 base pairs long. Estimate the size of the shortest DNA fragment from the crime scene. [1]

_____ base pairs

Further Biology (New Technologies) B7

7. Read this article about Tay–Sachs disease.

> Tay–Sachs disease is a fatal genetic disorder caused by a single mutation on a gene on chromosome 15 and the trait is homozygous recessive. A baby with Tay–Sachs disease has no signs or symptoms of the disease at birth. However, 3 to 6 months after birth, symptoms start to show. The symptoms are caused by damage to the brain and nerve cells, caused by the build-up of fatty compounds. An early sign of the infantile form of Tay–Sachs is a red spot on the retina. Unfortunately the child will deteriorate and die around the age of 4.

(a) What does it mean when the trait is said to be **homozygous recessive**? [1]

(b) To find out whether a person carries the Tay–Sachs allele, they can undergo a genetic test. Read the following sentences, which describe the steps involved in genetic testing. Put a (ring) around the correct options. [4]

A sample of **DNA / RNA** is isolated from **red / white** blood cells. A gene **probe / protein** with a UV-fluorescing marker is added to the sample. UV light is then used to identify if the **allele / antigen** is present.

8. Read this newspaper article.

> ## A New Type of Stem Cell
>
> In 2010, scientists were able to take certain adult cells and alter the DNA so that they became pluripotent. Pluripotency means that the cells can develop into any type of cell.
>
> Scientists believe that this will change the face of medicine because degenerative diseases, such as arthritis, thalassemia and Parkinson's disease, may finally be cured.
>
> The new type of stem cells are called induced pluripotent stem cells, or iPS cells.
>
> There are a number of arguments as to why it is preferable to use iPS cells rather than the alternatives. However, a lot of research still needs to be undertaken before the use of iPS cells becomes commonplace.

(a) What other type of stem cell is pluripotent? [1]

(b) Give an **ethical** reason why it is preferable to use iPS cells rather than the alternatives. [1]

B7 Further Biology (New Technologies)

(c) Why do the adult body cells have to be induced to become iPS cells? [2]

(d) A potential problem with iPS cells is that they can become carcinogenic. Explain the arguments **for** and **against** using iPS cells to treat incurable disorders and suggest why people may still choose to have iPS cell treatments.

The quality of written communication will be assessed in your answer to this question. [6]

(e) Two people with the same condition may reach different decisions about having the treatment. Suggest why this may be so. [1]

[Total: .... / 22]

Notes

Notes